The Alternate World

If the Red Sox hadn't traded Babe Ruth in 1920, then:

- Ted Williams is still alive, unfrozen and known by his nickname, "Mr. October."

- Joe DiMaggio is still alive and known only as "Mr. Monroe."

- There is no designated hitter or artificial turf.

- John Lennon never met Yoko and the Beatles stayed together.

- Mickey Mantle lived and is the director emeritus of Alcoholics Anonymous.

- George Steinbrenner was fired after losing his ship company in a hostile takeover and now works as a greeter at a Wal-Mart in Conneaut, Ohio.

- Sated by Boston's many championships, Red Sox fanatic Ben Affleck never made a movie.

Jim Caple is a senior writer for ESPN.com, where he writes regular baseball and humor columns. He formerly reported on sports for the *Seattle Post-Intelligencer* and *Pioneer Press* (St. Paul). He lives in Newcastle, Washington.

The Devil Wears Pinstripes

George
Steinbrenner,
the Satans of Swat,
and the Curse of A-Rod

JIM CAPLE

A PLUME BOOK

PLUME
Published by Penguin Group
Penguin Group (USA) Inc., 375 Hudson Street, New York, New York 10014, U.S.A.
Penguin Group (Canada), 10 Alcorn Avenue, Toronto, Ontario, Canada M4V 3B2
(a division of Pearson Penguin Canada Inc.)
Penguin Books Ltd., 80 Strand, London WC2R 0RL, England
Penguin Ireland, 25 St. Stephen's Green, Dublin 2, Ireland (a division of Penguin Books Ltd.)
Penguin Group (Australia), 250 Camberwell Road, Camberwell, Victoria 3124, Australia
(a division of Pearson Australia Group Pty. Ltd.)
Penguin Books India Pvt. Ltd., 11 Community Centre, Panchsheel Park,
New Delhi – 110 017, India
Penguin Books (NZ), cnr Airborne and Rosedale Roads, Albany,
Auckland 1310, New Zealand (a division of Pearson New Zealand Ltd.)
Penguin Books (South Africa) (Pty.) Ltd., 24 Sturdee Avenue, Rosebank,
Johannesburg 2196, South Africa

Penguin Books Ltd., Registered Offices: 80 Strand, London WC2R 0RL, England

First published by Plume, a member of Penguin Group (USA) Inc.

First Printing, March 2005
10 9 8 7 6 5 4 3 2 1

"The Yankees Clubhouse" on pp. 18–19 and "The House That Rudy Would Have Built" on
pp. 144–145 copyright © Kurt Snibbe.
Chapter opener illustration copyright © Arnold Roth.
Part of chapter 2 as well as portions of chapters 3 and 9 originally appeared in a different
version online at ESPN.com.

Ⓟ REGISTERED TRADEMARK—MARCA REGISTRADA

LIBRARY OF CONGRESS CATALOGING-IN-PUBLICATION DATA
  Caple, Jim
    The devil wears pinstripes : George Steinbrenner, the satans of swat, and the curse of A-
Rod / Jim Caple.
      p. cm.
    ISBN 0-452-28598-4
    I. New York Yankees (Baseball team)—History.   2. Steinbrenner, George M.
(George Michael), 1930–   I. Title.
  GV875.N4C27 2005
  796.357'64097471—dc22   2004024435

Printed in the United States of America
Set in Clearface Regular and OptiSport-Script

CONTENTS

To my mother and father, Jeannette and Verle Caple, who took me to my Little League games, let me stay up late listening to games, brought me to the library to read the out-of-town sports pages and taught me to root for the underdog.

And to all the Yankees fans who made this book necessary.

ACKNOWLEDGMENTS

This book would not have been written had Stacey Glick, a great literary agent and a pathetic Mets fan, not read some of my ESPN.com pieces and tracked me down to suggest that I write a book on the Yankees. She then represented me so well as my agent that I'll be surprised if Alex Rodriguez doesn't drop Scott Boras and sign her up. (Please, Yankees fans, do not blame her for this book—she has a rough enough time rooting for the Mets as it is.)

My editor at Plume, Gary Brozek, made this book far easier than I ever dreamed possible by piecing together a hodgepodge of fact, fiction and pure fantasy and somehow turning it all into a single readable work.

My many editors at ESPN.com were always encouraging, particularly Kevin Jackson and Jay Lovinger. Even though Jay roots for the Yankees and was busy with his own book, he was especially helpful in reading early chapters and offering suggestions. So, too, was Jon Scher, the baseball editor at *ESPN the Magazine*. (And don't worry, Jon, my next project is not a book on the Duke Blue Devils.) Dave Schoenfield and Joy Russo, meanwhile, went beyond the call of duty and friendship when they allowed me to set up shop in their home so I could watch twenty-four consecutive hours of the YES Network (sorry about the broken TV screen). ESPN.com Page 2 editor Michael

Knisley also helped out by loosening my ankle-irons when deadlines approached.

Kurt Snibbe once again bowled me over with two extraordinary cartoons—"Yankees World" and "Inside the Yankees Clubhouse"—he drew especially for this book. You can catch his work regularly in the *Orange County Register* and on ESPN.com.

Rod Mar, good friend and late-night Instant Messenger mate, provided needed inspiration for several items in this book. He's not only the best sports photographer in the country, he's a talented and funny writer who gives me more ideas than I deserve. John Sisko, an extraordinary sculptor, likewise was there to listen to me work out ideas for the book.

Fellow ESPN writers Jayson Stark, Jerry Crasnick, Rob Neyer, Buster Olney (whose terrific book, *The Last Night of the Yankee Dynasty,* is available in bookstores now) and Tim Kurkjian were generous with their vast knowledge and help as always. Sharing baseball coverage with them for ESPN.com is like being the backup catcher on the 1927 Yankees. Darren Rovell, ESPN's unparalleled sports business reporter, took a break from his competitive-eating training regimen to help me out with information regarding Yankees finances. Scott Miller, my good friend since our days covering the Twins, provided needed encouragement at timely moments. In addition to providing helpful advice, my sister Kathy blazed the trail.

Finally, I must salute my wife, my best friend and my muse, Vicki Schuman, for enduring my many late nights of writing, my use of the laptop on our vacations and her chore of editing. I don't know if this book would have been possible without you, but I definitely know it wouldn't have been worthwhile.

Bennett Cert, my deceased publisher, always sensed that there was something about him I didn't like, something that kept us from being good friends. He finally asked me what it was, and I told him I could never be comfortable with anyone who was a Yankee fan, which he was. I told him I thought there was something fundamentally sick about being affiliated with the Yankees.

—James Michener

October Surprise

Now they finally know how they always made everyone else feel. For most of their history, the Yankees have bullied around the rest of baseball, signing the best players, generating the most money, winning the most games and giving everyone else atomic wedgies.

Not during the 2004 American League championship series. Despite the highest payroll in the league, despite the highest-paid player in the game and despite every advantage this side of swinging bats named Wonderboy, the Yankees became the first team in baseball history to take a 3–0 lead in a best-of-seven postseason series and still lose. There couldn't have been a more stunning reversal of form short of Tim McCarver becoming a street mime.

Finally, the Yankees felt the pain they so often mercilessly inflicted on so many others. Finally, another team's curse turned into their own angry curses ("That @#$&-ing A-Rod couldn't get the ball out of the infield!"). Finally, they had to spend the World Series the same way as everyone else, trying to watch it on TV in between all those annoying camera shots of Fox network "celebrities."

Finally, the Yankees were losers.

As soon as Ruben Sierra grounded to second base for the final out, street vendors slashed prices in half on "Who's Your Daddy" T-shirts.

New York fans fell as silent as if they had seen Don Zimmer dancing in his underwear. Barge traffic on the River Styx backed up due to pack ice. And as a security precaution, major league officials ordered riot police to surround George Steinbrenner's luxury suite in case of an eruption.

If the collapse had happened to any other team, you would have felt sorry. But it didn't happen to anyone else. It happened to the Yankees, the legendary Bronx Bombers, baseball's Evil Empire. And boy, was it wonderful.

Remember the end of the first *Star Wars*, when Darth Vader is zeroing in on Luke Skywalker and his proton torpedoes are locked in on Luke's X-wing fighter and he's about to blast him to smithereens? And then at the last possible moment Han Solo and Chewbacca fly in out of nowhere to save the day by zapping Darth's tie-fighter and sending him spinning into space? And how Luke uses the Force to hit the target and the Rebels beat the Empire and that soaring John Williams theme music blares while everyone celebrates and Leia hands out the medals and we see R2-D2 all shiny and fixed up? Remember how great that felt?

That's what the Yankees collapse felt like, an event so emotionally stirring that mothers across the country tied yellow ribbons around old oak trees while sailors searched for nurses to kiss in Times Square.

There was only one problem. We're all going to pay for it. Yankees fans included.

You see, even while celebrating New York's great defeat, we knew, *we just knew,* that as surely as *The Empire Strikes Back* followed *Star Wars*, as surely as the villainy of Darth Vader was eventually surpassed by the hideous plague that was Jar-Jar Binks, Steinbrenner would follow up with a sequel of his own. Even as we laughed at the Yankees ("Where did you learn to run the bases, A-Rod? Filene's?"), we knew that Steinbrenner was already releasing the hounds, sending Brian Cashman to Niger to purchase enriched uranium to restart the team's nuclear program and hiring bounty hunter Boba Fett to capture Carlos Beltran or any other available free agent and bring them to the Bronx sealed in carbonite.

Even Yankees fans so devout they send their Paul O'Neill replica jersey in for dry cleaning every Monday had reason to worry, knowing that Steinbrenner would become so desperate he would invest in more miserable SOBs like Kevin Brown or decide that he had left Joe Torre in charge too long or generally make personnel moves that would force fans to pay ever higher moral costs for their favorite team to keep winning.

So savor the joy and the satisfaction that October brought as long as you possibly can. As the following chapters make clear, these emotions won't last. It's only a matter of time. If there is one thing that we've learned about the Yankees, they always return, bigger, more evil and much more expensive than ever.

Count on it. The Devil will be back, wearing pinstripes and bearing a bill in his hand. And not only will there be hell to pay, Ticket-Master will tack on a 20 percent convenience fee.

CHAPTER 1

The Evil Empire

On December 26, 1919—a date which will live in infamy—New York Yankees owner Jacob Ruppert purchased Babe Ruth from the Boston Red Sox for $24 worth of trinkets and beads. He then immediately hired Halliburton to begin construction on the Death Star.

No, wait. That's not right. Ruppert actually gave Red Sox owner Harry Frazee $100,000 in confederate bonds, and Halliburton wasn't hired to build the Death Star until 1973, when George Steinbrenner bought the Yankees. What Ruppert actually ordered was the construction of Yankee Stadium, and as every baseball fan knows, Ruth built the ballpark single-handedly from scratch in between swatting home runs on demand from hospitalized orphans.

Or something like that. You can never be too sure about Yankees legends.

The specifics of the transaction are of little consequence anyway; what is of real importance is that this date marks the official origin of the Evil Empire. Prior to that date, the Yankees had yet to play in a single World Series and were relatively harmless to Americans as a whole. Vaccination shots weren't even necessary. Then came Ruth, and the Yankees not only reached the World Series the second season with him in uniform, they went on to play in it another thirty-eight times as well.

Our nation has never truly recovered.

We've developed a vaccine for influenza, eradicated smallpox, and not only cured polio but invented the remote control so you wouldn't have to walk to the TV to change the channels anyway. But year after year, from one generation to the next, the Yankees remain a national plague. Other teams rise and fall (remember when the Kansas City Royals were good?), but except for frustratingly brief periods, the Yankees have been as constant a baseball annoyance as organ music.

The Yankees have been such a dominant, hated and feared empire that the only thing missing is an annual May Day parade of tanks, nuclear missiles and All-Star shortstops past Steinbrenner, Rudy Giuliani and the rest of the politburo.

They are the team of Ruth, Lou Gehrig, Joe DiMaggio, Mickey Mantle and now Alex Rodriguez. They've played in nearly 40 percent of the World Series and have won one in every four. They won so consistently in the immediate postwar years—playing in fourteen of sixteen World Series during one stretch and twenty-two of twenty-nine during another—that they nearly destroyed interest in baseball. Average league attendance was nearly 1.4 million in 1948, the year before the Yankees began their longest championship run. When that dynasty ended with a losing season in 1965, average AL attendance was down to 886,000 fans, or roughly what Boston draws for a championship celebration riot.

The Yankees have won so often and produced so many great players that the very thought of beating them inspired a musical about a man who sold his soul to the devil in order to defeat them—and it was a hit again on Broadway four decades after its debut. They've changed their uniforms less often than the Catholic Church, wearing their CEO pinstripes for ninety years. Their Tiffany-designed interlocking NY logo is as internationally a recognized icon of America as the golden arches and Donald Trump's hair, one that reflects tradition, stability, pride and arrogance.

God, don't you just hate them?

Chicago columnist Mike Royko wrote that hating the Yankees is as American as pizza pie, unwed mothers and cheating on your income tax. "Rooting for the Yankees," comedian Joe E. Brown said in the 1950s, "is like rooting for U.S. Steel." Sigh. If only that were true. U.S. Steel reported $350 million in losses in one quarter alone during 2003. The Yankees just keep on winning the American League East season after miserable season. They're no longer like U.S. Steel, they're like Wal-Mart with nuclear warheads.

It's not just their winning that drives us nuts, it's the way they win. They are so arrogant that they can strut while in a catcher's squat. Other teams have their pitchers practice covering first base during spring training. The Yankees are so cocky, *their* fundamental drills include the proper ways for piling on the mound, spraying champagne in the clubhouse and waving to fans in a ticker-tape parade (although, apparently they do not include how to run to first base). They think the world revolves around Yankee Stadium so much that they thought Tampa Bay should have to forfeit a game in 2004 when the Devil Rays were prevented from flying to New York in time for a scheduled start due to Hurricane Frances, a Category 4 storm that killed at least thirty in Florida, knocked out power to 6 million and forced mass evacuations.

Gehrig would have been there on time, you wimps.

They are as enduring—and despised—a fixture in American life as income taxes. When Hollywood filmed the classic movie about Little League baseball, *The Bad News Bears,* it chose the Yankees as the archrival that audiences would instantly recognize as the symbol of everything dark and evil. And that was a dozen years after the real Yankees had most recently been in the postseason.

The Yankees in the movie were just little kids, but you could just imagine them brushing past fans in the Bronx and refusing to sign autographs as they swaggered around in those familiar pinstripes. Vic Morrow, who always played deliciously nasty SOBs, portrayed Yankees manager Roy Turner, one of the great sports villains of all time. Smug and overbearing, he gives the Bears the oldest, worst equipment while reserving only the best gear for his precious Yankees. He beats his son, Joey, and gives out such helpful pieces of advice as, "Why don't you do everyone a favor and get the hell out of the league?"

You just know that in some darkened theater, Steinbrenner was smiling and nodding his head and whispering to his assistant, "Smithers, this man belongs in our organization."

The Yankees beat the Bears to win the championship, of course, and receive a trophy so enormous not even Rickey Henderson would wear it around his neck. They then "congratulate" the Bears on their second-place finish and apologize for their loutish behavior in such a condescending manner that Bears shortstop Tanner Boyle responds with the treasured words that are as richly patriotic and meaningful to Americans as "We find these truths to be self-evident . . ."

"Hey, Yankees!" Tanner shouts. "You can take your apology, and your trophy, and shove it straight up your ass!"

Joey Turner Tells His Side of the Story

"Sure, I know nobody liked us Yankees much, but let me tell you, those Bad News Bears weren't exactly the lovable underdogs everyone thought they were, either.

"Take Engelberg, or as I liked to call him, Engelpuke. Everyone thought I was the bad guy because I supposedly threw a pitch at his head, but I was just trying to establish the inside part of the plate and my cut fastball got away from me a little. And what everyone ignored when they were busy hounding me out of the league was that Engelpuke's father lied on his birth certificate. Yeah, just like with that Almonte kid in the Little League World Series a couple years ago. Engelpuke wasn't twelve years old, he was sixteen. I know, because he forced my bicycle off the road with his station wagon on the way to a game one day. So I can't say I was surprised when he was indicted for his part in the Enron scandal.

"Everyone knew Coach Buttermaker was a drunk, but he wasn't the only substance abuser the Bears had. You know why Timmy Lupus was such a booger-eating spaz, he couldn't field or hit? Because he was higher than a kite the whole season. Yeah, he was the biggest stoner in the league. If he wasn't smoking pot he was sniffing airplane glue. Hell, I once saw him try to get a buzz by drinking Neat's Foot Oil, that crap you're supposed to rub on your glove. He's in jail now—he was one of the main suppliers in the Pittsburgh drug trials.

"Then there was Amanda Whurlitzer. Yeah, right—'Amanda.' I'll let you in on a little secret. I ran into 'Amanda' in college, only by then she was going by her real name: Manny. She wasn't a girl, just a guy with a nice curveball who liked to dress up like a dame. Last I heard, he and Rudi Stein were interior decorators living together in the Castro District.

"And Kelly Leak. Shit. You think he hit all those home runs without a little help from the pharmacy? Give me a break. He was juiced up on steroids the whole time he was in the league. Dianabol, THG, andro, catnip, you name it, if he thought it would add distance to his hitting, he put it into his body.

"How could I tell he was on the juice? Easy. Acne."

The Evil Empire: Behind the Music

Sure, the Yankees are a great team to follow if all you care about is winning. But those of us with at least an ounce of decency in our bodies know better.

The Yankees pat themselves on the back so often, they need a full-time team of orthopedic surgeons to repair their rotator cuffs, but their biggest stars are far from the mythic heroes the Yankees and the New York media constantly present them as. Ruth, their greatest hero, went into the stands to fight a heckler and, as Robert Creamer chronicles in his biography, stood on the dugout shaking his fist and hollering at fans, "Come on down and fight! Anyone wants to fight, come down on the field! Ah, you're all yellow!" He was a notorious heavy drinker and womanizer, and his celebrated "bellyache heard round the world" in 1925 likely was either caused by a venereal disease or tainted liquor (or, quite possibly, both). What was the Babe really like? Consider this anecdote, which the late New York sportswriter Richards Vidmer recalled in Jerome Holtzman's *No Cheering in the Press Box.*

According to Vidmer, the Babe asked him to stop by his hotel room one night. After drinking and chatting about thirty minutes, Vidmer said he saw a shadow at the bedroom door and asked Ruth whether he had a woman in there. Ruth replied that he did and Vidmer apologized for interrupting.

No, Ruth replied. "That's why I wanted you to come up. I thought I'd need a rest."

Funny, but that story didn't get written up like the one about Babe hitting a home run for sick little Johnny Sylvester.

First baseman Hal Chase, one of the most notorious players in baseball history, was so widely regarded as accepting bets on baseball that New York manager George Stallings accused him of lying down in games. (Chase was eventually banned for life for his involvement in the 1919 Black Sox scandal.) DiMaggio was a miserable tightwad who slapped around Marilyn Monroe. Mantle was an alcoholic whose eventual liver cancer was about as surprising as the Marlboro Man coming down with lung cancer. Steve Howe and Darryl Strawberry were drug addicts. And don't even bring up Billy Martin.

Compared to their owners, however, the Yankees players are altar boys.

Steinbrenner might have been convicted for illegal campaign contributions shortly after he bought the team, but he was just doing his best to fit in as a Yankees owner. The original owners, Frank Farrell and Bill Devery, were connected to Tammany Hall, one of the most corrupt political rings in American history. Farrell ran illegal gambling parlors and an off-track betting syndicate. Devery, often described as one of the most corrupt police chiefs in New York City history, was even worse. He was involved in so much graft and so many protection rackets that Teddy Roosevelt said Devery "represented in the Police Department all that I had warred against while commissioner." He was so open about his crooked ways that, according to *A Battle for the Soul of New York* by Warren Sloat, Devery told muckraker Lincoln Steffens:

> You know so much more than I do, especially crooked knowledge about crooked men and things, I got to ask you a question that's been bothering me some of late. What I want to know is, have you noticed any stray graft running around loose that I have overlooked?

"Colonel" Ruppert, who (along with the impossibly named Tillinghast L'Hommedieu Huston) bought the team from Farrell and Devery in 1915, had Tammany Hall connections as well and based his dubious military title on an honorary appointment in the National Guard. In his book *The Diamond in the Bronx,* Neil Sullivan reports that Del Webb, who owned the team with Dan Topping from 1945 to 1964, made part of his massive fortune building World War II projects that included internment camps for Japanese Americans, and had casino ties with such infamous mob figures as Bugsy Siegel and Meyer Lansky.

None of those actions, however, was as grievous as the one CBS was responsible for when it bought the team: putting *Hogan's Heroes* on the air.

While Steinbrenner is infamous for firing managers, he is merely following his predecessors' examples—the Yankees have always changed managers more frequently than they change the hot dogs on the concession stand grills. Every team fires the manager when the team loses, of course, but the Yankees also fire them when they win. They fired Casey Stengel in 1960 after he had just guided the Yankees to their tenth World Series in the past twelve seasons. They fired Yogi Berra in 1964 after he won ninety-nine games and took them to the World Series in his first year as manager. And Steinbrenner has fired three managers after they got the Yankees to the postseason.

Not that the Yankees would always describe it as a firing. When Topping announced Stengel's departure at a press conference, he asked the manager, "You are retiring of your own volition, aren't you, Mr. Stengel?" To which Casey replied, "Boys, I'm not retiring—I've just been fired. . . . I commenced winning pennants when I got here but I didn't commence getting any younger. . . . I'll never make the mistake of being seventy years old again."

The managers aren't the only ones to suffer under New York's ownership. Convinced that the best way to keep a player motivated was to keep him hungry, the Yankees placed their teams on a strict low-carbohydrate, low-fat, low-sugar, low-dairy, low-sodium and most importantly low-salary diet that would have had Gandhi screaming for a pay raise and a Double Whopper with extra bacon and cheese.

Sure, the Yankees famously paid Ruth $80,000 in 1930, or $5,000 more than President Hoover ("I had a better year than he did," the Babe said in what was probably an apocryphal story), but they also cut his salary $5,000 two years later after he hit .373 with 46 home runs, reached base nearly half the time, scored 149 runs and drove in 163 runs. By 1934, they had cut his 1930 salary in half, to $37,000, after he hit only 34 home runs (second in the league). Even granting that this was the depth of the Depression, this was an astoundingly shabby way to treat the most important player in the team's history. And they were even worse to Gehrig. Considered one of the game's immortals and a true gentleman to boot, Gehrig played every single game for the Yankees for fifteen years but they never paid him as much as $40,000.

Hey, we would like to give you more, but remember that one day you went home early from spring training? And that time you cut the cheese on the team bus and pretended it was someone else? What kind of an example would we be setting if we rewarded that kind of behavior with a raise?

If the Yankees treated their two biggest stars this poorly, they mercilessly exploited the players who didn't have the good fortune of being regarded among the greatest in the game's history. The only thing missing from the Yankees' Dickensian approach to their players was a pasty-faced orphan begging general managers Ed Barrow and George Weiss for another bowl of gruel.

Weiss acted as if the players were taking their paychecks directly out of his wallet, which in a way they were. According to David Halberstam, ownership gave Weiss a percentage of the money he saved in the team's budget, and he pinched his pennies so tight that Abraham Lincoln should have had him arrested for sexual assault. When "negotiating" with his players, Weiss stubbornly insisted that they consider their World Series shares as part of their regular salaries. He even offered Mickey Mantle a $5,000 pay cut after he won his second consecutive MVP award in 1957.

What? Again, no Cy Young Award? You should feel lucky I don't send you back to Triple A. Now, get out of my office, you slacker, before I throw you out on your ass.

This mean-spirited, tightfisted approach lasted after Weiss was gone.

"My very first contract with the Yankees, after I made the team in spring training, was signed two minutes before they sang the national anthem on opening day," former Yankees pitcher Jim Bouton says. "We were just about to take the field and the general manager, Roy Hamey, tells me to stay behind. He puts the paper down on the table and says, 'Sign this contract.' I start reading it and he says, 'Don't read it. It's the same everyone else signs.'"

After Bouton went 21-7 for the Yankees in 1963, general manager Ralph Houk offered him a $15,500 contract, and when he refused to sign, Houk warned that the offer would be lowered $100 every day he held out. Bouton, like everyone, eventually gave in.

"You sign it because if you don't, they could make it so you never played again," he says. "You're a young kid, it's your big chance, your parents are in the stands and you're suddenly going to be a troublemaker? Imagine leaving the clubhouse and telling your parents why you're not pitching. 'Oh, I didn't like the contract.' It's not going to happen."

The Yankees were so cheap that they resisted Cap Day—"Do you think I want every kid in this city walking around with a Yankees cap?" Weiss once asked—until attendance plummeted so much in the sixties that the team had no choice but to try luring fans back with such promotions. Even then they couldn't stop themselves from charging twenty-five cents apiece for the "giveaway" T-shirts.

They were worse than cheap, though. With a lineup that regularly features whites, Latinos, African Americans and Japanese players, today's Yankees are as racially and culturally diverse as the No. 7 subway train, but back in the Weiss era, their integration record was roughly equal to Mississippi's.

It's important to stress that prior to Jackie Robinson's debut in 1947, every team was guilty of segregation, but the Yankees were more active in maintaining the color barrier than others (though, admittedly, not quite as active as the Red Sox, who should have been managed by George Wallace). By the end of Robinson's eighth season in 1954, he, Roy Campanella and Willie Mays had combined to win four MVP awards . . . and the Yankees clubhouse still was as white as the cast of *Friends*.

Elston Howard finally cracked the Yankee color barrier in 1955, but he still was the only African American in the daily lineup when he won the MVP award in 1963, the same season the Dodgers swept the Yankees in the World Series with a team that included five blacks in their regular lineup. The Yankees won fourteen pennants from 1949 to 1964, but their discrimination policy ultimately proved devastating for the franchise—the club's reluctance to sign players of color was a contributing factor to their mid-'60s collapse.

Not that that should be considered justification for racial discrimination.

"Help Us, Obi-Wan Kenobi, You're Our Only Hope"

When Yankees fans brag about their team's success over the years (and not even the 2004 postseason could silence them for long), they always conveniently forget the enormous advantage New York has held over almost every other team in the game. If the Yankees have won more games than anyone else, it's partially because they're usually spotted a couple runs thanks to their location.

Other teams have revenue streams, the Yankees have the Mississippi River at flood stage. And that was true before Steinbrenner bought the team, too—the Yankees have *always* had an unfair economic advantage over their rivals.

In the years before broadcast revenues came into play, New York's vast population and Yankee Stadium's capacity gave them attendance advantages over every other team in the league. At a time when attendance was essentially a team's only source of real revenue, the Yankees owned a stadium more than twice as large as Sportsman's Park in St. Louis and played in a city with a population that was more than eight times that of St. Louis (which had two teams to support). You think it's hard for a small-market team to compete now? Consider the 1930s, when the Yankees once drew more fans in one day (83,000 in 1938) than the St. Louis Browns drew in an entire season (80,922 in 1935). The Yankees drew nearly as many fans in 1930 (1,169,230) as the Browns drew that entire *decade* (1,184,075).

That great a revenue disparity would have left Bud Selig foaming at the mouth so uncontrollably he would have had to be put down with a tranquilizer gun.

And remember, this was at a time when there was no free agency, no player agents and virtually no negotiating leverage for a player. In theory, the Yankees didn't have to pay their players any more than the Browns paid theirs. The additional revenue allowed the Yankees to continually build their farm system, enabling them to sign and develop more players with no amateur draft to offset this advantage.

The Yankees were so dominant and controlled so many players in their system that in 1953 their minor league pitcher George Toolson filed suit against the team so that they would let him play with another team, and the case went all the way to the Supreme Court. That case gave the Yankees the unique distinction of having a player petition the Supreme Court so that he didn't have to play for them. Unfortunately, the Court ruled against Toolson and he never pitched for the Yankees or anyone else again.

Even having the Supreme Court batting cleanup wasn't enough for the Yankees. Already the rulers of the sport's largest and richest market, they spun their web to snare a Midwestern market: Kansas City.

In the 1950s, the Yankees exploited a shady relationship with the owner of the Kansas City Athletics that provided enormous payoffs at the bank and on the field. At best the deal was a cozy one for the Yankees; at worst it was incestuous enough that it should have been banned everywhere other than remote areas of Tennessee. The arrangement was so involved that it makes the plot to *The Matrix* seem simple, but the key fact is that it resulted in a business partner of the Yankees' owners buying the Athletics, and then the two teams exchanging fifty-nine players in a five-year span. Most of these trades were so lopsided for New York that Cleveland general manager Hank Greenberg complained, "It must be nice to have your own farm system in the same league." The most infamous of these deals were the 1957 trade that sent Clete Boyer and Bobby Shantz to New York for seven nobodies and the 1959 trade that sent Roger Maris to New York for the immortal Marvelous Marv Throneberry and fading players Hank Bauer and Don Larsen—none of whom was still playing in Kansas City after 1961 when Maris broke Ruth's single-season home run record.

It was like having Texas Rangers owner Tom Hicks give you his best player every year, with the added benefit of not having to negotiate with agent Scott Boras.

The Yankees' dominance, however, eventually wound up working against them. The 1950s are often labeled as baseball's golden era, but in reality the gold was restricted to New York—at least one (and often two) of the three New York teams played in every World Series that decade except 1959. The Yankees won so often that their own fans started losing interest in the game. Attendance began declining in the early 1960s when fans preferred to watch the Mets lose rather than the Yankees win.

Crippled by the lack of minorities in the system and then by inept ownership when CBS bought the club in 1964, the Yankees dynasty crumbled and a great peace settled over the land. Beginning in 1965, a different team won the World Series every season for eight years—

and not one of them was the Yankees. All seemed possible during this time. The Beatles released *Sgt. Pepper's Lonely Hearts Club Band* and *Abbey Road*, man walked on the moon and the Mets performed the last miracle confirmed by the Vatican, the Amazing Randi and Dionne Warwick's Psychic Friends Network.

And then came 1973, the year Steinbrenner bought the Yankees, dispatched his Black Riders on the Shire to recover the World Championship Ring and seized control of Middle-Earth and the American League. The Yankees Third Reich had begun and the dark times had returned to baseball.

The Death Star Is Fully Operational

It was a different era in 1973. For one thing, the Carpenters, Helen Reddy and Donny and Marie all had top-ten singles that year (what the hell was wrong with us?). More importantly, the Yankees payroll was less than $2 million, or about what A-Rod makes pulling on his stirrup socks. They drew less than a million fans the season prior to Steinbrenner's arrival and they were literally paying a radio station to carry their games. It was a situation so loaded with opportunity that even a complete moron could turn things around.

Enter Steinbrenner.

The Boss may be so manically petty that he has ordered players to get haircuts, but he knows how to make money. He also built the Yankees into an empire so powerful and vast that it ought to have a seat on the United Nations Security Council.

Steinbrenner brought attendance back to the 2 million mark and returned the Yankees to the World Series in just three years. By 1980, he nearly tripled the attendance mark from when he bought the team. Then in 1988 he truly took the team into its own personal orbit by signing a historic broadcasting deal with Madison Square Garden that paid him half a billion dollars over the next twelve years.

How much local TV revenue do the Yankees receive now? That's difficult to say without access to the team's financial books, a building full of accountants and an MIT mainframe. Even major league officials would like to know the amount. When the MSG TV deal ran out, the Yankees simply started their own twenty-four-hour network, forcing *Yankeeography* upon defenseless viewers and thereby answering the question, "Is there anything more excruciating than watching non-stop *Little House on the Prairie* reruns on the Hallmark Network?"

Next on Yankeeography: *Horace Clarke.*

The broadcast revenues alone would put the Yankees far ahead of the league, but Steinbrenner's financial philosophy is No Coin Left Behind the Sofa Cushion. The Yankees signed a deal with Adidas in 1997 that paid them $93 million just to put the company's logo on top of the dugout and in other select areas of the stadium. (Fortunately there is no truth to the rumor that Steinbrenner tried to have the logo tattooed to Don Zimmer's skull—it's believed he was instead planning to rent that space out to Budweiser.)

Meanwhile, the Yankees' $29 average ticket price was second in the league to only the Red Sox in 2004 (despite working overtime to close the gap by raising the price of a field box to $80 and the price of an infield box from $52 to $70). That translates into more than $100 million in revenue from ticket sales. Throw in profits from concessions and parking and the Yankees take in enough each year to practically fund NASA.

Always in search of lebensraum, the Yankees expanded their reach to across the Atlantic in 2001 by partnering with Manchester United, soccer's equivalent of the Yankees, in a move that was akin to Hannibal Lecter hiring Norman Bates to run the building maintenance department. They crossed the Pacific two years later by allying with the Yomiuri Giants, the most successful franchise in Japanese sports, in a deal that greased the skids for them to sign home run champ Hideki Matsui just weeks later.

Unfortunately for everyone competing against him, Steinbrenner spends these riches so recklessly that it's as if he hires Brown & Root to rebuild the Yankees roster each winter. Just when you think the

Yankees might finally be showing their age and becoming vulnerable, he trades for the game's most expensive player or signs Roy Hobbs.

By 2004, New York's payroll had risen to about $186 million. That doesn't count its obligations to players no longer with the team, but it still was almost $160 million more than division rival Tampa Bay, about $60 million more than the second-highest payroll in baseball and as much as the bottom five teams combined. Just as was the case years ago, the Yankees can afford to buy whatever players they need. From Ruth to Reggie to A-Rod, the Yankees' secret to success has always been the same: open the wallet and pull out the cash.

Always looking for more money, the Yankees now have plans for a new stadium and all its vast revenue opportunities. They are so insatiable, they could eat the entire menu at the Cheesecake Factory and still ask for second helpings. Heck, when they traveled to Japan for two games in 2004, they flew in their own groundskeeper, even though they played the games in the Tokyo Dome, which has artificial turf.

This then is the true Curse of A-Rod. Not that Rodriguez will *never* play in the World Series, but that the Yankees will *always* have the financial resources available to sign whoever they want, making it that much tougher on everyone else to compete.

The Evil Empire will never, ever be satisfied, not even when they are so rich that they can replace their bullpen carts with fully loaded Cadillac Escalades.

The Awful Truth

And now, here's the really disturbing, sobering part.

The reality is that as much as we all hate the Yankees, we *need* them. They are an integral part of baseball's circle of life, making the game a richer, fuller and more entertaining sport.

"Definitely. Not just historically but in an ongoing way, it's a good thing when the flagship franchises are of championship caliber," broadcaster Bob Costas says. "It would be a good thing if the Boston

Celtics or the Dallas Cowboys were champions. It's good when Notre Dame is winning.

"The Yankees have contributed a lot of the lore to the game. Some of the most beloved and poignant figures have been Yankees—Ruth, Gehrig, Mantle, and I would include DiMaggio, too. What mitigates against the resentment many have for the Yankees is the fact that almost all the players in the Joe Torre era, and Torre himself, have been classy and unassuming people."

The Yankees provide the mark against which we can gauge our own clubs, they provide our teams a standard to aspire to and most importantly they provide us a common enemy to root against each year. How many fans outside of Arizona would have cared about the Diamondbacks winning the 2001 World Series had they not beaten the Yankees? How many fans outside of Florida would have cared about the Marlins winning the 2003 World Series had they not beaten the Yankees? (For that matter, how many fans *in* Florida would have cared?) How much sweeter was Boston's historic comeback in 2004 because it was against the Yankees? Hell, Boston's entire economy would collapse if it couldn't sell "Yankees Suck" T-shirts.

Atlanta won thirteen consecutive division titles and went to the World Series five times in that span, but did anyone hate them? No. Fans were incredibly bored by Atlanta and its repetitive World Series losses, but they didn't hate them.

No one likes to admit it but deep down everyone wants to beat the Yankees in the playoffs or in the World Series to validate their own October experience.

"There is an indescribable mystique about the franchise," Hall of Famer Paul Molitor says. "Even though they went through a long period where they didn't win from 1981 to 1996, with the ballpark and everything, there was always something very special about that team."

"If you beat the Yankees, you feel like you've accomplished something," manager Joe Torre says. "I know as a player, we would play the Yankees in spring training, even in the years when they weren't winning championships, and there was something the pinstripes stood for that made you feel a lot better when you beat that ball club. There's no question that people test themselves against us.

"Whether you like us or hate us—and I don't think there are many who fall in between—they still are curious, they still want to come out."

Compare the Yankees to the Los Angeles Lakers, a great basketball dynasty. The Lakers have won the NBA championship nine times, including eight times since Dyan Cannon's first face-lift (or about twice as many titles as the Yankees have won in that same period). They play in the nation's second-largest market. They are the team of Wilt, Kareem, Magic, Shaq and Kobe. They have a highly visible, highly annoying celebrity fan base. And yet when Gary Payton and Karl Malone joined the team during the 2003 off-season, there was no national outcry that Jerry Buss was buying another championship, no national anger that the Lakers were stockpiling all the best players, no national push for a Constitutional amendment banning the triangle offense. People simply don't hate the Lakers enough to care. (Or maybe it's just that Buss gives fans the Laker Girls shaking their cans to "Hey Ya!" while Steinbrenner only gives us the grounds crew raking the infield to "Y.M.C.A.")

The same is true for Notre Dame football, Duke basketball or any of the other great sports dynasties. Their victories just don't make people put their local sports talk radio station on speed dial.

Not so the Yankees. There is no team fans love to hate more than the Yankees. When they come to town, it's a civic event, like a visit by Monday Night Football or Oprah. Hard-core, casual and nonfans alike want to see them. The Yankees not only led the majors in home attendance in 2003 and 2004, they led the majors in road attendance as well, which they usually do by a healthy margin. As disturbing as the A-Rod trade was for many fans—the Yankees getting the league's best player was like Bill Gates winning the Powerball—it stirred overall interest in the game, causing blood pressures to rise higher than Yosemite Sam's.

"It's better to be hated," Derek Jeter says, "than to have people not even care about you."

He's right. The Yankees connect generations. We may have nothing else in common with our fathers but we know that they hated the Yankees too, and that their fathers hated the Yankees and that their fathers hated the Yankees and on and on all the way back to Luke and Anakin Skywalker.

Mike Moorby runs Yankeeshater.com, a Web site dedicated to all things anti-Yankees, and even he sees the Yankees' value to baseball. "You take the black hat out of the picture and you've got nothing. You've got no drama," he says. "If you could poll Red Sox fans and ask them if they could drop a blanket and have the Yankees disappear tomorrow, would they want that—and they wouldn't."

Not having the Yankees in baseball would be like not having the Nazis in *Casablanca*.

Which, in a way, is a good thing, if only because they aren't going anywhere. Even after momentary setbacks such as the 2004 choke, you know they will be back to beat your team. Maybe not today, maybe not tomorrow, but soon, and for the rest of your life.

Damn them.

CHAPTER 2

The Unofficial Yankees Timeline

The New York media has spread so many legends about the Yankees dynasty that it's hard to know fact from fiction. In fact, there are times when it's difficult to believe all this has transpired in barely a century of Yankees baseball. . . .

January 9, 1903: Tammany Hall–connected "businessmen" Frank Farrell and Bill Devery purchase the defunct Baltimore Orioles and relocate the team to New York and rename them the Highlanders. In their first official move as owners, they sign left-handed relief specialist John Franco.

January 10, 1903: Columnists and small-market owners accuse New York of trying to buy the pennant.

April 11, 1912: After New York adds bleachers to Hilltop Park, Tammany Hall "businessmen" Farrell and Devery extend their former career practices by demanding protection money from opposing outfielders.

April 22, 1913: New York officially renames the team the Yankees, forcing Boston vendors to sell their entire stock of "Highlanders Suck!" T-shirts at a huge loss.

December 26, 1919: In what is generally considered the blackest day in the city's history, generations of Boston fans are doomed to nearly nine decades of frustration, agony and psychological torture—construction begins on the Big Dig.

Meanwhile, in the most infamous and lopsided deal in American sports history, the Red Sox sell Babe Ruth and their immortal soul to New York in exchange for the deed to the Brooklyn Bridge.

April–September 1920: Ruth hits fifty-four home runs to shatter the single-season record and earn two dozen nicknames, including the Bambino, the Sultan of Swat, the Consigliore of Crunch, the Lieutenant Governor of Lumber, the Chief Operating Officer of Bash, the Senior Vice-President in Charge of Purchasing and Slugging Percentage, the Right Honorable Ensign of Clout and the Notary Public of Horsehide.

April 18, 1923: Affectionately known as the House That Ruth Built, Yankee Stadium opens, setting the stage for many additional New York structures, such as the Apartment That Rizzuto Built, the Townhome That Skowron Erected, the Duplex That Horace Clarke Leased and the Low-Income Housing Complex That Pepitone Gutted and Sold Off as Luxury Condominiums.

October 15, 1923: After the Yankees beat the Giants to win their first world championship, columnists and small-market owners complain that there needs to be better revenue sharing because the Yankees win the World Series every year.

April 1925: Ruth misses the first two months of the season when he accidentally eats a hot dog from the Yankee Stadium concession stand.

June 1, 1925: In a very poor career decision, Wally Pipp calls in sick and stays home to lie on the couch all day and watch old movies on TV.

October 1, 1926: Inspired by a promise from Ruth that he'll hit a home run for him, little Jeffrey Maier rises from his hospital bed, attends the World Series and catches the Babe's home run by reaching onto the field and taking it out of right fielder Tony Tarasco's glove.

May 20, 1927: Charles Lindbergh astounds the world when he accomplishes the long-sought goal of aviation duration—a solo flight around Ruth's waist.

May 16, 1928: Billy Martin is born. He is bottle-fed by Ballantine.

July 4, 1930: The unsuspecting victim of a witches' coven, Rosemary Woodhouse gives birth to the son of Satan, George M. Steinbrenner III.

August 12, 1931: Steinbrenner utters his first words, telling his nanny, "You're fired."

October 1, 1932: In one of the most dramatic moments in World Series history, the Babe steps to the plate and points to center field, where the cast of Fox's *Arrested Development* just happens to be sitting.

May 30, 1939: Lou Gehrig ends his playing streak at 2,130 games and Mayo Clinic doctors deliver the most obvious diagnosis in medical history, telling him that he has Lou Gehrig's disease. It is only one of the many ailments named in honor of a Yankees superstar. Others include Epstein-Berra Syndrome, Non-Knoblauch's Lymphoma and, of course, Mickey Pox.

July 17, 1941: Joe DiMaggio's amazing record streak finally ends when he signs an autograph without attorney Morris Engleberg charging for it.

May 28, 1944: Profitable Yankees souvenir sales are guaranteed for the next eight decades when Rudy Giuliani is born.

April 12, 1947: Yankees co-owner Dan Topping changes his mind after a drunken agreement to trade DiMaggio to the Red Sox for Ted Williams's frozen head.

October 5, 1951: Mickey Mantle suffers the first of several debilitating knee injuries in Game 2 of the World Series when he trips over his pile of empties.

January 14, 1954: DiMaggio marries Marilyn Monroe, and upon consummating the marriage delivers the most famous line in baseball history: "Tonight, I consider myself the luckiest man on the face of the earth."

October 8, 1954: The Giants sweep Cleveland in four games when the Yankees vote to not win the pennant, "just to see what it's like."

May 5, 1955: The musical *Damn Yankees* opens on Broadway, telling the story of a frustrated fan who sells his soul to the devil in order to pay his cable bill for the YES Network.

May 16, 1957: Billy Martin wins the WBC lightweight championship and runs his record to 13–0 with a TKO at the Copacabana.

October 13, 1960: After beating the Pirates 12–0 in Game 6 of the World Series, the Yankees douse manager Casey Stengel with the Gatorade jug, pop the corks on the champagne and then forget to show up for Game 7.

October 1, 1961: After a long, emotionally ravaging summer, Roger Maris endures another indignity when he hits his record-breaking sixty-first home run and his family hugs Mark McGwire instead.

November 4, 1964: The Yankees dynasty crumbles when CBS officially assumes control of the team and, in a cost-saving move, fires Yogi and replaces him as manager with Gomer Pyle.

October 3, 1966: After the Yankees finish in last place for the first time in fifty-four years, Steinbrenner announces that he is firing manager Ralph Houk. The dismissal is ignored when it is pointed out that Steinbrenner won't own the team for another seven years.

March 2, 1970: Jim Bouton becomes a Yankees pariah when he writes his bestselling tell-all diary, *Mickey and the Yankees Were a Bunch of Pricks*.

December 8, 1972: Fritz Peterson and Mike Kekich swap wives but are unable to complete the entire trade when Luis Polonia claims their daughters on waivers.

January 3, 1973: The Lamb breaks the seventh seal, the Angel blows the seventh trumpet, earthquakes ravage the globe, California sinks into the Pacific, the sun disappears from the sky, the moon runs crimson, the magnetic poles reverse, the pestilence-ridden undead roam the earth and Steinbrenner buys the Yankees.

December 20, 1973: Steinbrenner is suspended for two years after he and six other burglars are caught breaking into Democratic headquarters at the Watergate Hotel.

June 26, 1974: With the planet Krypton disintegrating, Jor-El places his infant son in a rocket ship and sends him to Earth, where Charles and Dorothy Jeter name the boy Derek and raise him as their own in the Michigan town of Smallville.

April 16, 1976: Renovated Yankee Stadium opens with Rudy May throwing out the first pitch and bleacher fan Mark Rooney throwing out the first battery. The renovation enlarges the stadium enough that it is able to hold the ego of free agent Reggie Jackson.

October 18, 1977: Reggie slams three home runs in Game 6 of the World Series and headline writers dub him "Mr. October," adding

him to the pantheon of Yankees greats such as "Hank Bauer—
Mr. February," "Elston Howard—Mr. Late-December," "Kevin
Maas—Mr. July 13th" and "Ed Whitson—Miss April."

October 2, 1978: Bucky Dent officially becomes the leading cause
of clinical depression, schizophrenia and obsessive-compulsive
disorders in Boston.

October 18, 1981: With no thought to his personal safety,
Steinbrenner courageously brings order to a hotel elevator
by repeatedly punching two drunks with his face.

October 20, 1981: After losing the final game of the World Series,
the Yankees won't reach the postseason for fourteen years, leaving
columnists and small-market owners nothing to complain about.

July 24, 1983: Umpires nullify George Brett's home run after manager Billy Martin protests that he was using Sammy Sosa's bat.

April 28, 1985: Steinbrenner fires Yogi for being a nice man who
everybody likes.

May 14, 1987: Steinbrenner hires Howard Spira to call up Dave
Winfield to ask if he has Prince Albert in the can.

June 6, 1990: Six months after the death of Billy Martin, Steinbrenner orders the body dug up and hires him as manager for the sixth
time. There is no apparent difference between the dead Martin and
the manager he replaces, Stump Merrill.

July 1, 1990: Andy Hawkins pitches a no-hitter but loses when the
White Sox score four unearned runs after Yankees infielders
repeatedly trip on Don Mattingly's long hair.

July 31, 1990: After investigating the Spira-Winfield affair, baseball
places Steinbrenner on double-secret probation.

October 6, 1991: The Yankees finish in last place for the first time in twenty-five years. Congress declares a national holiday.

June 2, 1992: Yankees scouts sign Jeter after discovering him turning double plays with *Daily Planet* second baseman Jimmy Olsen in the Metropolis newspaper softball league.

August 11, 1994: In what can only be described as a miracle that inspires renewed worldwide belief in a higher power, the first-place Yankees lose a chance for their first title since 1978 when the players strike ends the baseball season.

September 23, 1994: Episode 4 in Ken Burns's nine-part documentary *Baseball* accidentally gives the impression that baseball is played west of New York City. Burns apologizes for the mistake and promises it will be corrected for the home video release.

October 26, 1996: The Yankees celebrate their first world championship in eighteen years by voting Jeffrey Maier a full World Series share.

May 17, 1998: In the finest performance of his career, David Wells retires twenty-seven consecutive beers without spilling a drop.

November 15, 1998: After a very sick DiMaggio enters the hospital's intensive care unit, Morris Engleberg instructs reporters that he is to be referred to as "The Greatest Dying Ballplayer" in their stories.

February 18, 1999: The Yankees acquire five-time Cy Young winner Roger Clemens. Boston responds by changing the greeting on the club's phone lines from "Home of the 1918 World Series champions" to "Yankees Suck!"

August 12, 2000: History is made, play is halted and a special ceremony is held when the umpire calls a strike and Paul O'Neill doesn't bitch about the call.

October 21, 2000: Game 1 of the first Subway World Series in forty-four years is marred when an enraged Clemens rips the head off a cocker spaniel puppy and throws the furry body at Mike Piazza.

October 12, 2001: In Game 3 of the division series with Oakland, Jeter returns from a Justice League of America meeting just in time to throw Jeremy Giambi out at home plate.

March 13, 2002: The Yankees release outfielder Ruben Rivera after they catch him stealing Joe Torre's silverware.

April 2, 2002: After a year of hype and anticipation, the twenty-four-hour YES Network debuts in well over a dozen homes.

February 12, 2003: President Bush warns the United Nations that the Yankees have weapons of mass destruction and insists on preemptive action.

April 1, 2003: The Yankees celebrate their one hundredth anniversary by unveiling the commemorative shoulder patches they'll wear throughout the upcoming season: "2003 World Champions."

July 31, 2003: Steinbrenner gears up for the stretch drive by trading Drew Henson for the entire National League.

October 11, 2003: Game 3 of the Yankees–Red Sox championship series is marred when Pedro Martinez knees public address announcer Bob Sheppard in the crotch and throws him to the Twiground. New York reliever Jeff Nelson and right fielder Karim Garcia retaliate by assaulting Cub Scout troop 714.

January 20, 2004: The Yankees human resources department informs Clemens that due to recent career decisions, he is not eligible to begin drawing on his 401(k).

February 15, 2004: Steinbrenner trades for MVP shortstop Alex Rodriguez and moves him to third base and then buys up all sixty-four teams in the office NCAA basketball tournament pool.

April 29, 2004: Jeter extends his slump to 0 for 32 after he mistakenly corks his bat with kryptonite.

July 18, 2004: Jason Giambi and Kevin Brown lose weight and are left too weak to play after they contract a parasite eating from the Shea Stadium concession stands.

September 2, 2004: Brown is lost for the season when he breaks his hand defending Steinbrenner from two drunks in an elevator.

September 24, 2004: After Pedro Martinez discloses that "the Yankees are my Daddies" following yet another loss, Red Sox president Larry Lucchino files suit against Steinbrenner, demanding $60.4 million in delinquent child support payments.

October 16, 2004: Steinbrenner celebrates the Yankees' 19–8 victory over the Red Sox in Game 3 of the American League championship series by hanging a banner above their dugout that reads "Mission Accomplished."

October 21, 2004: The Red Sox beat the Yankees in Game 7 to complete the most dramatic comeback in baseball history. Steinbrenner responds by insisting that the Red Sox have to win by two, and begins selling tickets for Game 8.

October 23, 2004: Steinbrenner sues baseball for calling the games between the Red Sox and Cardinals the "World Series," claiming that the Yankees own the copyright. Meanwhile, ticket sales are disappointing at bunting-draped Yankee Stadium for fans to see Challenger the eagle fly, the grounds crew to drag the infield to "Y.M.C.A." and Ronan Tynan to perform "God Bless America."

"I consider myself . . ."

Thirty words shorter that Lincoln's Gettysburg Address, Lou Gehrig's simple yet eloquent 244-word farewell is one of the most famous speeches in American history, recognizable to anyone who has ever seen *Pride of the Yankees* or been forced to watch the YES Network for more than two hours.

"Fans," Gehrig began that emotional day in 1939, "for the past two weeks, you have been reading about what a bad break I got. Yet, today, I consider myself the luckiest man on the face of this earth. I have been in ballparks seventeen years and have never received anything but kindness and encouragement from you fans."

Gehrig then went on to praise his employers, his managers, his parents, his wife and even his mother-in-law (was this guy for real?), and then finished by saying, "I might have had a bad break, but I have an awful lot to live for."

Of course, Gehrig was a splendid, Ivy League–educated man. The speech might have gone a little differently had other famous Yankees delivered it:

Babe Ruth: "Today, I consider myself the hungriest man on the face of the earth. Can someone get me a dozen hot dogs? And while you're at it, round me up some broads. Hell, if I'm gonna die anyway, I might as well enjoy myself. Come to think of it, you sure this ALS thing isn't another venereal disease?"

Yogi Berra: "When they told me I got Lou Gehrig's disease, I asked them what disease Lou had, and how could I catch it from him if we had never even been in the same room. At first I didn't think I was too sick because when the doctors x-rayed my brain, they didn't find anything. Then the doctor tells me I have six months left, but he won't tell me which ones. All he tells me is that it got late early. I asked my wife where we go when we die and she said no one goes to heaven anymore because it's too crowded.

So in closing, I just want to thank everyone who made this disease necessary and that I ain't over 'til I'm over."

Joe DiMaggio: "I may have had a bad break, but today, I still consider myself the greatest living ballplayer. And I just want to know why everyone keeps calling this illness Lou Gehrig's disease. I've instructed my lawyer, Morris Engleberg, to file suit against the Mayo Clinic, requiring its doctors to immediately rename this disease after me, with all appropriate royalties going to my estate."

Don Zimmer: "Yeah, I got a bad break with this Lou Gehrig's disease but I don't consider that makes me any unluckier than when I was playing winter ball in Cuba and I got lost walking home after a game one night and wound up getting captured by Castro and his guerrilla forces in the jungles outside Havana. Castro was a big baseball fan and he recognized me and wanted to show off his arm. So they gave me a bat and he marched off sixty feet, six inches and started pitching. I hate to admit it but even in his army boots he had a pretty good fastball for a communist. But finally he hung a curveball and I belted it over a grove of coconut trees. That's when Castro got pretty angry and ordered my execution. One of his lieutenants shot me in the head point-blank and they left me for dead. But the bullet didn't penetrate the steel plate in my head so I was only knocked unconscious for a couple hours. After I came to, I wandered back to Havana and got to the stadium. I was thirty minutes late for batting practice though, so they fined me fifty dollars—I swear, sometimes the general managers could be worse than the communists. . . . Now, what the hell was I talking about?"

Reggie Jackson: "Today, I consider myself the greatest man on the face of the earth."

Billy Martin: "Today, I consider myself the unluckiest man on the face of the earth, next to Mickey Rivers. Liver cancer I could understand, but Lou Gehrig's disease? What the hell did I do to deserve that? If anyone should get this stinking disease, it's that dirty lying SOB Reggie. Not that you would have noticed if he had ALS, the way he stumbled around in the outfield. I swear, he was the worst outfielder in the league even when he tried, which wasn't very often. And selfish? Hell, he made Munson look like Mother @$%#ing Teresa. I should have kicked that miserable @$%#'s ass when I had the chance. And I still could, even with the shitty disease. You don't think I can? Just try me, you little piece of dogshit, try me."

Roger Clemens: "I like the way you talk, mmmm-hhhhmmm. Some people call it a Kaiser blade, I call it a slingblade. Mmmm-hmmmm. I don't reckon I got no reason to kill nobody. Mmmm-hmmmm. . . ."

David Wells: "Today, I consider myself the thirstiest man on the face of the earth. Can anyone get me a six-pack of Heinekens?"

George Steinbrenner: "Fire Cashman."

CHAPTER 3

Darth Steinbrenner

George Michael Steinbrenner III was born a long time ago in a galaxy far, far away—but very near the Cleveland suburb of Tatooine—where his difficult and demanding father taught him to run the family shipbuilding business, wield a light saber and harness the Force to cloud minds and bend free agents to his will. After receiving multiple student deferments from serving in the Clone Wars, Steinbrenner dabbled in minor league sports and musicals, then flew his tie-fighter to New York, where he bought the Yankees from CBC in January 1973.

Steinbrenner was part of a fifteen-person partnership that included John DeLorean, the man whose chief claims to fame were being set up by the government on cocaine charges and designing the car that Michael J. Fox drove in *Back to the Future*, and Nelson Bunker Hunt, who created an international investment crisis in the late '70s by trying to corner the world's silver market. The presence of those two investors alone answers the age-old question, "Could there possibly be a worse owner than George Steinbrenner?" The group bought the Yankees for just $10 million, which not only was less than CBS paid for the team a decade earlier but was $800,000 less than the Cleveland Indians had just been sold for. It also was less than the Yankees would pay closer Mariano Rivera to pitch 78⅔ innings in 2004, though we can safely say Steinbrenner had a little something to do with the escalation in player salaries in the ensuing thirty-one years.

"We plan absentee ownership," Steinbrenner assured reporters at the press conference announcing the purchase. "We're not going to pretend we're something we aren't. I'll stick to building ships. I won't be active in the day-to-day operations at all."

That's one of those quotes that sounds too deliciously good to be anything but apocryphal, like Dylan Thomas's supposed last words: "I've had eighteen straight whiskies, I think that's the record. . . ." But Steinbrenner *really* did say that, adding, "I can't spread myself so thin. I've got enough problems with the shipping industry. . . . I'd be silly trying to run a ball club, too."

And the very next day he stole all the Christmas presents in Whoville and dumped them from the top of Mount Crumpet.

There I go again, playing fast and loose with the facts. Steinbrenner did not steal Christmas from Whoville the next day. That happened later. First, he was convicted of a felony for illegally donating $100,000 to President Nixon's reelection slush fund. Commissioner Bowie Kuhn suspended him from baseball for two years in the only worthwhile contribution Kuhn ever made to baseball.

Steinbrenner remained in power, however, just long enough to hire Robert Merrill to sing at the wedding of his daughter, Princess Leia, to Han Solo. Whoops, sorry. I got carried away again. What he really did was take his first step toward dethroning Charlie Finley as the most boorish, meddling owner in baseball history. He called a press conference a week before Christmas 1973 to announce the hiring of the manager who had just won his second consecutive World Series and who would soon lead the Yankees back to the October glory that was the Fatherland's just and rightful due: Dick Williams.

There was just one slight problem. Williams was still under contract with the world champion Oakland Athletics.

So what the hell, Steinbrenner hired Bill Virdon instead. And like it really mattered in those days who Steinbrenner hired as manager. None of them lasted long enough to order cable TV for the office and still be around by the time the guy came around to install it. During the 1992 presidential campaign, the U.S. unemployment rate rose to 7.5 percent, but as the Republicans pointed out, that rate was actually a much more tolerable 6.2 percent if you didn't count ex-Yankees managers. From 1978 to 1992, the Yankees changed managers seventeen times, with Steinbrenner firing Billy Martin alone five times. As Martin said in 1983 shortly before Steinbrenner fired him for the third time, "All I know is, I pass people on the street these days, and they don't know whether to say hello or say good-bye."

Of course, the real tragedy of all that bloodletting is Steinbrenner never made the one move that would have endeared him to even his staunchest enemies. He didn't kill Jar Jar Binks when he had the chance.

 ### *The Pink Slip*

Steinbrenner's managerial moves are legendary, but like a Monet painting of water lilies, sometimes the full majesty can be appreciated only by taking a couple steps back and looking at the whole picture. Take a deep breath—here goes.

1973: Hires Dick Williams, then hires Bill Virdon to replace him when it is discovered that Williams still works for the Athletics.

1975: Fires Virdon and hires Billy Martin to replace him.

1978: Forces Billy to "resign" in July for saying of Reggie Jackson and Steinbrenner, "One's a born liar and the other is convicted." Replaces him with Bob Lemon, then announces four days later that Billy will return as manager in 1980.

1979: Loses patience, replaces Lemon with Billy. Fires Billy in October and replaces him with Dick Howser.

1980: Forces Howser to "resign" for winning only 103 games in his first season as a major league manager. Replaces him with Gene Michael. Howser's advice to Michael: "(Have) a strong stomach and a nice contract."

1981: Fires Michael in September after the Yankees have already clinched a playoff spot and replaces him with Lemon.

1982: Claims in spring training that "Bob Lemon's going to be our manager all year. You can bet on it. I don't care if we come in last. I swear on my heart that he'll be my manager all season." Fires Lemon fourteen games into the season and replaces him with Michael. Fires Michael three months later and replaces him with Clyde King.

1983: Replaces King in January with Billy. Fires Billy in December and replaces him with Yogi Berra.

1985: Begins spring training by telling reporters that "Yogi will be the manager this year. I said the same thing last year and I'm saying it again this year. A bad start will not affect Yogi's status." Fires Yogi sixteen games into the season and replaces him with Billy. Yogi vows never to return to Yankee Stadium as long as Steinbrenner owns the team. Fires Billy in October after New York wins ninety-seven games and replaces him with Lou Piniella.

1987: Replaces Piniella in October with Billy.

1988: Fires Billy in June and replaces him with Piniella. Fires Piniella in October and replaces him with Dallas Green, promising that he will manage the entire 1989 season.

1989: Fires Green in August and replaces him with Bucky Dent.

1990: Fires Dent in June and replaces him with Stump Merrill.

1991: Stump is fired and replaced by Buck Showalter.

1995: Fires Showalter after he leads the Yankees to their first postseason in fourteen years. Replaces him with Joe Torre.

1996: Gives Torre relatively free rein while Steinbrenner moves to Bedford Falls where he concentrates on foreclosing the Bailey Bros. Building and Loan.

The only thing worse than being fired by Darth Steinbrenner, of course, is being hired by him. Working for Steinbrenner is like working as a security guard on the set of *Jerry Springer*, only with less dignity.

You know how beaten down new parents look after they've spent six consecutive months waking up every forty-five minutes to hold, feed and comfort their crying babies? Well, that's what working for Steinbrenner is like ("Hush little baby, don't you cry, mockingbird gonna make Giambi's knee all right"), except that unlike a newborn, he weighs more than two hundred pounds and knows how to operate the speed dial on his phone.

As Lou Piniella told *Sports Illustrated*'s Tom Verducci in 2004: "George is a great guy unless you have to work for him."

Steinbrenner has occasionally sought lie detector tests of his employees after leaks to the media. When the 2002 basic agreement raised the luxury tax and revenue sharing on the richest teams, Steinbrenner responded by firing two scouts and cutting the hours for Yankee Stadium elevator operators. He also considered eliminating dental coverage for 150 employees to save an estimated $100,000. This at a time when he was increasing the team's payroll more than $30 million and paying Bubba Trammell $2.5 million to bat fifty-five times for him.

He fired PR director Rob Butcher in 1995 because he made the mistake of being home in Ohio for a Christmas vacation—a vacation Steinbrenner had approved—when the Yankees re-signed David

Cone. (In total fairness, George might also have been cranky because Marley's ghost had kept him awake the previous night.)

"As I was getting on the plane, Cone signed. And George called the office and I wasn't there," Butcher remembers. "When I landed, I called into the office and they said, 'George is pissed. We signed David Cone and you weren't around.' So I called his home in Tampa and I said, 'Mr. Steinbrenner, congratulations—you got David Cone.' You know, trying to butter him up. He says, 'Where were you, young man?' I said, 'I was home.' He said, 'You don't go home when we do something like this.' I said, 'Don't worry, I'll be back tomorrow for the press conference.' And he said, 'No, no, I really don't want you to come back at all.'"

Butcher knew from the stories that Steinbrenner often says things like this but that you just go back into work the next day and everything is fine. So he flew back to New York and went to Yankee Stadium the next day. Only to be told that Steinbrenner meant it—he wasn't wanted anymore. So he flew back to Ohio, and a week later he received a call from Steinbrenner. He said, "I would like you to come back. I think you've learned your lesson."

I think you've learned your lesson.

"I've never forgotten that part," Butcher says. "To this minute, I've never gotten over him saying, 'I think you've learned your lesson.' Because the one thing about his employees is they work their asses off for him. And I did. And I didn't do anything that I needed to learn a lesson for. I went home for a vacation that he was aware of.

"That's just the way he treated people sometimes. It was really the first time he treated me like that. He had threatened me before that, but it was always, 'If I see that in the newspaper again you're going to be finding another job' type stuff.

"From that entire ordeal, I've never gotten over 'I think you've learned your lesson.' And I swore I'd never work for him again. And I won't."

The firing may have been the best thing to ever happen to Butcher. He's now the PR director for the Reds, the team he grew up rooting for. Yankees employees, meanwhile, are stuck working for a man capable of firing people for taking a Christmas vacation.

Steinbrenner is such a micromanager that, as Bill Madden and Moss Klein relate in *Damned Yankees*, he once called Piniella out of his office in spring training and took him off to the side. Explaining that he was deeply troubled over the number of free passes that were being used for Yankees spring training games, Steinbrenner told his general manager to hide behind a bush and see who was using the free passes. "I didn't stay there very long," Piniella remembers. Another time, Steinbrenner instructed Piniella to go to Houston to scout a player, and in order not to be noticed to sit in the bleachers wearing a raincoat. The Astros, remember, played in the Astrodome at that time.

Sure, general manager Brian Cashman has a nearly unlimited budget and an office overlooking the Bronx, but he also has a no-win job. If Cashman signs the right free agents, swings the right trades and surrounds Torre with a world champion team, Steinbrenner takes the credit. If Steinbrenner insists on wasting money on overpriced broken-down has-beens like Jose Canseco, Cashman gets the blame when the players don't work out. Demonstrating his complete lack of respect, Steinbrenner wouldn't even allow his general manager to go to the winter meetings in recent years.

And heaven forbid the Mets do something to get the bigger headline in the morning papers.

When Jose Contreras fled Cuba in the winter of 2002 and Steinbrenner learned that the Red Sox were after the pitcher, he instructed his staff that if they lost Contreras to Boston, "You're done." (The Yankees traded the precious Contreras in 2004 after he had been a bust.)

Normally, a Yankees employee can at least look forward to the inevitable pink slip of freedom, but not in Cashman's case. In late 2003 the *New York Post* reported that Cashman was telling friends he had reached his limit with the Yankees and planned to leave the team after the 2004 season when his contract expired. So what did Steinbrenner do? The very next day he extended Cashman's contract another year.

Congratulations, son, I've extended your lease in Hell for all eternity. Would you like the heat turned up in your cell?

I worry about Cashman's long-term health. I've seen guys emerge from winter-long Dungeons & Dragons tournaments with a healthier pallor than he had during the 2003 World Series. He looked as if he hadn't eaten a vegetable or had a decent night's sleep since Nick Johnson had a full head of hair. And at least the Yankees beat the Red Sox and went to the World Series that year.

Then there is Torre, who has somehow remained one of the game's gentlemen despite working the past eight years for Steinbrenner. Torre broke into baseball when there were only sixteen teams in the majors. He was a teammate of Hank Aaron, Warren Spahn, Eddie Mathews and Bob Gibson. He made the All-Star team nine seasons, was a gold glove catcher and the 1971 MVP. He's managed four teams and twenty-four seasons, winning nearly 1,800 games, six pennants and four World Series. He beat cancer. He's one of the most respected men in baseball. He's been in the game as a player, manager or broadcaster almost since before Julio Franco entered puberty. He belongs in the Hall of Fame.

And he still has to take phone calls from a septuagenarian shipbuilder telling him that he should have pinch-hit for Bernie Williams in the eighth inning. It's like having the night manager at Hollywood Video criticize Spielberg for his camera angles.

"It's tougher to be a manager for him than general manager," says Piniella, who was both. "He told me when he made me the general manager, 'Come on up and join the rest of us second-guessers.'"

(Of course, there are some benefits to working for Steinbrenner. Housing costs and lengthy commutes are the bane of New Yorkers, but they are never a problem for Yankees employees. Steinbrenner supplies them with a cot in his office and a 10 percent discount at the famous Yankee Stadium concession stands, so they're able to live at the stadium. Thanks to George, employees face no strangling mortgage payments or escalating rents. No three-hour commutes. And there's hardly ever a line to use the restroom in the morning.)

To: ALL NEW YANKEE EMPLOYEES
FROM: GEORGE STEINBRENNER
RE: BENEFITS PACKAGE

Overtime: What's this? You haven't even started work and already you're looking for more money? Don't you realize that with the way they increased the asinine luxury tax in the new collective bargaining agreement I desperately need to keep my costs under control? I know your type. During the job interview you talk about what an honor it is to represent the Yankees and how hard you'll work for the team. Then we hire you, and the first thing you do is pass around a petition to start up a union. Well, I won't stand for it.

Besides, when I was your age, my employees at Steinbrenner Shipbuilding considered it a source of pride to work from dawn to dusk without so much as a cigarette break. They were embarrassed if they ever saw natural daylight. And that was exhausting, backbreaking work that you can't even begin to imagine, let alone perform. So quit your bitching. You don't get to the World Series by watching the clock, boy.

Vacation: Brother, you've really got some big brass ones, don't you? Asking for time off before you even punch your first time card. Listen, the only people I give vacations to are my most loyal boys in the shipyards, only it's not called a vacation, it's a layoff caused by the recession and excessive corporate taxes that lower the orders for ships. But there is never a recession in fielding a world champion, and, as long as there's work to be done, I expect you to work. You want to spend October vacationing in Aruba, go work for the Devil Rays.

Sick Leave: Now what? Like I'm supposed to pay you while you lie in bed sipping chicken soup and watching MTV videos? General Patton knew how to handle slackers like you—you don't need a day off, you need a kick in the ass. Listen up, pal. You don't win the World Series four times in five years from a sickbed. I remember when our shipbuilding employees wouldn't even think about phoning in sick until they were coughing up blood from having worked unprotected around asbestos for twenty years. And even then, I would dock them a day's pay and expect them to be in early the next day. If you want to call in sick, go work for the Blue Jays.

Medical Insurance: Hey, if you think you need medical coverage, try dealing with the migraines the insurance companies give me when they submit their estimates for a group rate. I used to think middle relievers were overpriced, but that's nothing compared with these bloodsuckers. Sorry, I just can't afford it anymore. And cutting medical coverage not only saved me a bundle in premium costs, it allowed me to lay off half the human resources department to boot. Look, I'm not your daddy. If you want health care coverage, go whine to that bitch Hillary Clinton about it . . . just don't waste my time or money. Besides, you looked fine when I hired you.

I'm not heartless, though. If your kid is in the hospital, I'll see about getting Giambi or Jeter to hit a home run for them. But he has to have something at least as serious as leukemia.

Dental Insurance: You've got to be kidding, right?

Pension/401(k) Benefits: Let me tell you something. Mickey Rivers was one of my favorite Yankees. Helped us return the team to dominance and restore its luster. Helped us win the World Series. Great player, great guy. But what has he done for me lately? He hasn't scored a run or caught a fly ball for us in years. Which is why I don't pay him anymore. So if I don't pay one of the greatest Yankees of all time after he left the team, why on Earth would I pay you? If you don't like it, go work for the Cubs. I'm running a world champion here, not Social Security.

Employee Stock Options: Do you ever stop? Listen, I sat through a two-year suspension from Bowie Kuhn. I outlasted that egotistical bastard Fay Vincent when he tried banning me for life. I wrote paychecks out to Danny Tartabull for four miserable years. And after all that you think I'm going to just give you part of the franchise for answering an ad in the classifieds? Don't hold your breath, pal. If you want your name in the *New York Post*, go buy the Mets, only you'll be buried on page 52 next to the word jumble— the back-page headline is reserved for me.

Now, get to work—we've got a pennant to win. And don't be lingering too long on those coffee breaks. Remember, I've got my eye on you.

Then there is Jeter. The Yankees have reached the postseason ever since they called him up from the Justice League of America. He's led them to eight AL East championships, six World Series and four world championships. He's a career .315 hitter, the highest average for a Yankee since DiMaggio. He's done everything short of stopping Lex Luthor from destroying California. And yet when his average slipped to .297 in 2002 (with 18 home runs, 124 runs and 75 RBIs), Steinbrenner ripped him for staying out too late and not devoting himself enough to the team.

And those guys have it easy compared to what Dave Winfield went through under Steinbrenner.

Winfield's problems began with the contract he signed in 1980, the biggest in baseball history—$16 million over ten years. It was a breathtaking price—remember, the entire club had cost $6 million less just seven years earlier—and you could practically see Steinbrenner's knees tremble as his serfs helped him down from the sedan chair to sign the contract.

Pay $16 million for one ballplayer? I'm probably going to end up regretting this but at least I've got the kind of superstar who will lead us back to the World Series and come through in the clutch like Reggie. But still—$16 million for one player is insane. Thank God it isn't a single penny more or I couldn't take it.

Oh, I'm sorry. Did I say $16 million? The deal actually turned out to be worth $23 million thanks to a cost-of-living escalator that Steinbrenner miscalculated. Over the next decade, salaries would rise dramatically, but thanks to the cost-of-living clause, Winfield still was one of the ten highest paid players in the game by the time he finally left the Yankees. He averaged 25 home runs, 100 RBIs and made the All-Star team every summer he played with New York, but this, of course, was not nearly good enough for Steinbrenner, who was frustrated that Winfield had gone 1 for 22 in the 1981 World Series and hadn't once sneaked out of the hospital to hit a home run that would cause the Yankee Stadium light towers to explode into fireworks. While the Yankees repeatedly failed to return to the World Series, Steinbrenner spent the following years trying to avoid his contractual payments to Winfield's charitable foundation, looking for dirt on Winfield, ridiculing him to the press ("Mr. May") and calling the outfielder at all hours of the night to ask whether his refrigerator was running.

It should be noted that among the lawyers he sicced on Winfield was Joe McCarthy's errand boy, the infamous Roy Cohn. The duplicitous shyster specialized in ruining lives and was a seven-time national SOB of the Year award winner. In other words, he was a perfect fit for the Yankees.

Steinbrenner had just gotten back from a meeting with the family consigliore, Tom Hagen, when he met up with the individual who would bring him to near ruin—the infamous gambler Paulie Walnuts, better known by his alias, Howard Spira. Heavily in debt to the mob for gambling debts, Spira rubbed himself between two rocks to shed his skin, then offered to dig up dirt on Winfield. *"I have it on good authority that Winfield never rewinds his movies all the way before returning them to the video store."* Most people wouldn't have had contact with Spira without rubber gloves, a surgical mask and a court order. Steinbrenner, however, gave him a check for $40,000. *"Thanks, Boss, you won't regret this. And for another $100,000, I'll rub out your brother Fredo."*

When word of the payoff reached major league offices, commissioner Fay Vincent placed a lifetime ban on Steinbrenner. Unfortunately, when issuing the ban Vincent forgot to use garlic and a wood stake. The lifetime ban lasted just two and a half years—though in fairness, that's almost eighteen in dog/owner years. Steinbrenner returned to baseball on March 1, 1993, drawing an estimated three hundred reporters and photographers amid rumors that he would arrive via helicopter.

"Some people say he's been going to parachuting school for the last six months," Wade Boggs told reporters.

A Yankee Doodle Dandy

Born on the Fourth of July, Steinbrenner loves elaborate displays of good old-fashioned American patriotism, and he is famous for swelling the chests of even Tim Robbins and Sean Penn when he sends Ronan Tynan to home plate during the seventh-inning stretch to sing those inspiring and patriotic lyrics:

Where did you come from, where did you go?
Where did you come from, Cotton Eye Joe?

Whoops. Those are the lyrics to "Cotton Eye Joe," which as everyone knows is as deep and traditional a part of New York City history as Cole Porter and Stephen Sondheim are a part of Dallas. I guess I just got confused listening to Tynan's extended dance version of "God Bless America" while watching the dancing Freedom Fries and Rockettes kick beneath a flyover by Challenger the eagle, a squadron of F-15 fighters and a giant Macy's balloon of the Statue of Liberty.

But Steinbrenner's patriotic pride extends far beyond such lavish productions or illegal campaign contributions. There is also his considerable work with the U.S. Olympic Committee. He served as the USOC vice president from 1989 to 1996 and left enough of a mark that the committee awards an annual George M. Steinbrenner Award (presented, I think, to the athlete who spends the most money on energy drinks and fires the most personal trainers). That's all great—good for him. Unfortunately, his devotion to the U.S. Olympic movement conveniently ends at the Yankee Stadium doorstep.

The U.S. baseball team had to finish in the top two at the 1999 Pan Am Games to qualify for a spot in the 2000 Olympics, so there was quite a push to get the best available minor leaguers on the roster. Many clubs were very cooperative—the Athletics provided Mark Mulder, the Twins provided Matthew LeCroy and J. C. Romero and the Merlins provided Brad Penny. But when USA Baseball wanted Nick Johnson, then a prospect with the Yankees AA team, Steinbrenner said no, you can't have him. New York, after all, needed Johnson just in case first baseman Tino Martinez got hurt and his backup also got hurt and the top first baseman at AAA Columbus also got hurt and the backup first baseman at AAA also got hurt—all in the exact same couple weeks when Johnson would be in Winnipeg. Unlikely occurrences perhaps, but you never know in baseball. Remember, a man named Stump once managed the Yankees.

The U.S. team barely beat Mexico in ten innings in the Pan Am semifinals that summer to qualify for the Olympics by the slimmest of margins. (Mexico returned the favor four years later by edging the U.S. team to prevent them from qualifying.) Even with a gold medal on the line in Sydney, the former USOC vice president shook his head when asked about allowing any Yankees prospects to compete for the United States.

"They said we couldn't take any of their players," says Bill Bavasi, who was cochair of the selection committee for Team USA at the time. "He gave us the boot."

Firmly ranked among our top ten national punch lines (alongside politicians, lawyers, reality TV stars and Michael Jackson), Steinbrenner has become such a caricature of himself that *Seinfeld* made him a recurring character when the storyline presented George Costanza with the longest-lasting job of his life, assistant traveling secretary for the Yankees. The *Seinfeld* Steinbrenner was a buffoon, the Sergeant Schulz of sports. He misidentified Costanza as a communist and sent him to Havana to sign a left-handed pitcher in one episode and rhapsodized over a calzone in another. The storyline finally ended when Steinbrenner assumed George was moonlighting for a chicken company and traded him for the chicken concessions at Yankee Stadium.

Chicken Owner: "Instead of hot dogs, chicken dogs. Instead of pretzels, chicken twists. Instead of beer, alcoholic chicken."

Steinbrenner: "How do you make that alcoholic chicken?"

Tyler: "Let it ferment, just like anything else."

"He was never really that funny. I don't remember him ever being exceptionally funny. He was always very serious," Butcher says. "What I'll always remember is how people were afraid of him. I always thought that was very sad. I mean, when he was at Yankee Stadium, I just remember people would say, 'George is here, George is here. The Boss is in the house.'"

Steinbrenner also hosted an episode of *Saturday Night Live* and appeared in two credit card commercials with Jeter. These things do not happen when you're the owner of the Kansas City Royals, and they certainly do not happen if you are merely the owner of a Cleveland shipping company. "I'll tell you another reason why I'm in baseball: ego," Steinbrenner told *Sports Illustrated* when he returned from his second exile. "Any owner would be lying if he didn't say ego played a major part. Do people say, 'There goes George Steinbrenner, the shipbuilder'? No. It's a little easier to get a table at a New York restaurant when you own the Yankees."

In other words, while it's infuriating for baseball fans and frustratingly expensive for opponents that Steinbrenner owns the Yankees, who cares! The man can get a table at Le Cirque on a Saturday night.

"These Are Not the Droids You're Looking For"

There is more hot air in Steinbrenner than in the big Macy's Thanksgiving Day Parade Underdog balloon. Saying he was overwhelmed by David Cone's $9 million signing bonus with the Royals in 1993, he told *Sports Illustrated* then that "Player compensation is as high as I hope to see it go. Baseball desperately, for its own sanity, must come to the same arrangement as the NBA and the NFL—a salary cap."

Steinbrenner calling for a salary cap is like Madonna advocating abstinence. Other owners have certainly contributed their fair share to rising payrolls, but no one has done so more significantly and more consistently than Steinbrenner.

The winter following his return, Steinbrenner began spending like a defense contractor contributing soft money to the Republican party in an election year. He raised the Yankees payroll to $47.5 million in 1994, highest in the majors, and raised it to $58.2 million in 1995 by trading for Cone and his "overwhelming" salary. The Yankees have had the highest payroll in baseball ever since (with the exception of 1998, when they were second to Baltimore), paying players more than *$1 billion* in the years since Steinbrenner called for a salary cap. The 2004 season payroll of nearly $190 million not only was the highest in the majors, it was nearly enough to buy a large beer at Yankee Stadium.

This is the most pressing problem with Steinbrenner. We can laugh about his ego and shake our heads at his treatment of employees, but the money he spends affects every other team. Every dollar he spends winds up inflating every other team's payroll because it absolutely raises the salaries players can command through arbitration (or the right of arbitration while negotiating a contract) and free agency. Forget the butterfly effect—when Steinbrenner signs Jason Giambi for $120 million, everyone winds up paying in the long run. This is not a mere Ronald Reagan trickle-down effect; this is Niagara Falls at full roar, Noah building an ark, the polar ice caps melting and David Wells sampling all the beers on tap.

Steinbrenner likes to consider his success a result of hard work and competitive zeal, investing repeatedly in his team. To a certain extent that is true—the Yankees purchased in 1973 were a shadow of their former selves, a mediocre team with lousy attendance (in short, America's dream) and he has returned them to their old dominance. But he can't take all the credit. Money can't do everything in baseball (the list of teams that have tried to buy a pennant only to fail miserably is a long one), but it certainly helps. And Steinbrenner has more available to him than anyone.

The Yankees can make a horrible mistake signing a player to an expensive contract (Hideki Irabu), shrug it off, find someone better and move on without losing a game in the standings. A bad contract can be devastating to a poorer team, slowing them down for years. Steinbrenner signs the likes of Ed Whitson, Steve Kemp, Dave Collins, Danny Tartabull, Irabu, Raul Mondesi and Contreras, and he just shrugs, writes off the bad investment and overcomes it by selling off the Joad family farm in Oklahoma.

Signing players he thinks will help his team is not enough for Steinbrenner, however. He'll sign players just to keep other teams from getting them (most notably in 2000 when he had the Yankees claim Canseco on waivers, much to Torre's dismay). The Yankees are so rich, they could afford to sign Jon Lieber in 2003 even though he wouldn't be able to pitch for at least a year and they already had seven starting pitchers.

Even as you read this, he is signing Little Leaguers to long-term contracts just in case they wind up in the majors.

The Verdict Is In

I can hear Steinbrenner's apologists. All this is ancient history. The man has changed. He has mellowed in old age. His days of randomly firing managers are a thing of the past. Indeed, he's become sentimental enough that he can be reduced to tears by commercials for the United Way or a long-distance carrier.

He's learned his lesson.

Well, I would certainly hope that in his seventies he's mellowed enough that he doesn't feel the need to fire one of baseball's best managers after watching him win six pennants and four world championships in eight years. But we're supposed to applaud Steinbrenner for not firing Torre? What's next, naming him executive of the year for flossing regularly?

Even when he gave Torre his latest contract extension, he just couldn't resist giving his manager a mild slap by saying, "You know he never was successful anywhere else he was, but when he got to New York he felt right at home and he did a great job for me and I owe him that." Of course, Steinbrenner was right to demean Torre's previous career. Until taking over as Yankee manager, all Torre had done was hit .297 lifetime and drive in 100 runs five times as a perennial All-Star and then manage Atlanta to its first division title in thirteen years in 1982. And evidently, managing the Mets for several years didn't count as a New York job, either.

But that's the thing about Steinbrenner. No one else is successful because of their own talent and hard work. In his eyes, they're only successful because he gave them the opportunity.

He is hated across the country—in *Sports Illustrated*'s national survey of sports, Steinbrenner was named as the No. 1 enemy by fans in eight states and No. 2 or 3 in twelve more. So the man who donated money to Nixon made the national enemies list in twenty of the fifty states. The hatred wasn't restricted to just New England, either (though those states were virtually unanimous)—Steinbrenner is hated in literally almost every corner of the country: Alaska, Maine and even his home state of Florida named him as Public Enemy No. 1. Not even Yankees fans know what to make of him—he finished second among the most hated sports figures in New York.

Look, I'll grant that Steinbrenner resurrected the Yankees franchise, saving it from the ruinous CBS ownership and returning it to its throne as the richest and most successful team in American sports. He's also a man who has dedicated himself to winning at all costs, a quality more owners could afford to have.

On the other hand, why does he have to be such a pain in the ass all the time?

A Tribute to George Steinbrenner

Here's a small collection of the things people have actually said over the years about the owner fans love to hate:

"The more we lose, the more Steinbrenner will fly in. And the more he flies, the better the chance there will be for a plane crash."

—former Yankees third baseman Graig Nettles

"If things go right, they're his teams. If things go wrong, they're your team. His favorite line is, 'I will never have a heart attack. I give them.'"

—former Yankees general manager Bob Watson

"What the hell does George know about being a Yankee? I'm a Yankee. I've worn the uniform. What the hell does he know?"

—Billy Martin

"It was a beautiful thing to behold, with all thirty-six oars working in unison."

—Jack Buck describing Steinbrenner's yacht

"I came into this game sane and I want to leave it sane."

—Don Baylor explaining why he didn't want
to manage for Steinbrenner

"Some teams are under the gun; we're under the thumb. The sweetest words to George are, 'Yes, Boss.' "

—Nettles again

"I tell George what I think and then I do what he tells me."

—Bob Lemon

"How do you know when George Steinbrenner is lying? When his lips are moving."

—Jerry Reinsdorf

"You come here and you play and you get no respect. They treat you like shit. They belittle your performance and make us look bad in the media. After they give you the money, it doesn't matter. They can do whatever they want. They think money is respect."

—Don Mattingly

"George doesn't know a fucking thing about the game of baseball. That's the bottom line."

—Dallas Green

"I don't know but if he does I'd like to be his owner."

—Gene Michael on whether Steinbrenner
could be a good manager

"Two things [Steinbrenner] knows nothing about are baseball and weight control."

—Nettles again

"I think the man is sick. I'll be honest with you. I'll only go back if George is gone. I'll never put on the Yankee uniform as long as he is there."

—Martin after his second firing

"It's actually sad because we were so close for twenty years or twenty-five years. But I'm a human being and I want to be treated like one. I didn't feel like I was. I've heard people say, 'He buys people back.' Here's one he can't buy back."

—Don Zimmer

"Working for George Steinbrenner was like doing two tours in Vietnam and not getting killed. It was the craziest two and a half years of my life. . . . Basically, it didn't matter what I did, George Steinbrenner was going to kick my ass. If I walked into his office with a briefcase full of a million dollars, he would have yelled at me that they weren't hundred-dollar bills, that they were twenties."

—Joe Perello, former Yankees VP for business development, in *Reveries* magazine

The Lord God of Baseball Giveth as Well as Taketh Away

A few of the nice things George Steinbrenner has said about some of his employees over the years:

"It astounds me. He can't catch, throw or hit. He should keep quiet until he can hit his weight, until his RBIs catch up with his age and until he can play third base like a normal person."

—on slumping third baseman Mike Pagliarulo

"He's a fat, pussy toad."

—on Japanese pitcher Hideki Irabu, whom he signed for $12.8 million

"They weren't even worth watching."

—on the Yankees, while offering fans a refund after a doubleheader loss to the White Sox

"They should have gone home with the vendors."
—on a bad game by pitchers Dave Righetti and Brian Fisher

"Where is Reggie Jackson? We need a Mr. October or a Mr. September. Winfield is Mr. May."
—on Dave Winfield after he got three hits
and drove in two runs in eleven at-bats
during a late-season series in 1985

"Well, a lot of people won't be happy with that, but that's good news for me."
—responding to a doctor who told him he
had only fainted and was going to be fine

CHAPTER 4

The Ten Yankees Who Drive Us Nuts

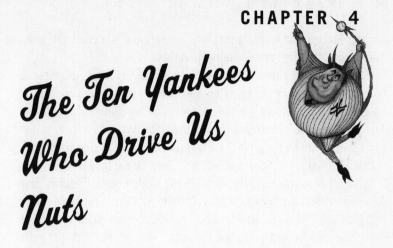

Baseball fans don't hate all the Yankees. Gehrig was one of the game's great gentlemen. Torre is such a great manager and such a decent guy that not even Steinbrenner has found reason to fire him. (Yet.) Even the most rabid Yankee Haters wouldn't have minded if Don Mattingly had been able to play in a World Series. Bernie Williams is a well-rounded and soft-spoken professional. Perhaps only Cary Grant ever looked as good in pinstripes as Jeter. And Yankees fans wouldn't be so damn annoying if they all were as restrained and dignified as Bob Sheppard.

It's just so many of the other Yankees who drive us nuts.

1. Billy Martin, infielder (1950–57), manager multiple times

The first time the Yankees got rid of Billy, they did so in part because of his behavior off the field. Now *that's* a feat. Getting traded from the Yankees for misbehavior off the field is like having Death Row Records rip up your contract because your lyrics are too coarse. The only honor more impressive than that would have been if the

Rolling Stones had kicked him out because he was a corrupting influence on Mick Jagger and Keith Richards.

Billy turned the drunken brawl into a true art form, working in liquor and left hooks the way Degas worked in pastels and oil, taking on everyone from marshmallow salesmen to his own pitchers if they dared walk into his preferred studio, the hotel bar.

"I don't want to fight you," Billy once said to a Reno sportswriter. "Little kids fight, men don't fight." And then he slugged him.

Like all true masters, Billy honed his skills over a lifetime, first drawing critical acclaim as a player, fighting Clint Courtney, Larry Doby and just about anybody who entered Yankee Stadium except Bob Sheppard. Billy also broke Chicago Cubs pitcher Jim Brewer's jaw in a fight that led to a nine-year lawsuit and a $10,000 settlement, but it was as a manager where he found his true medium. He was so feisty he once was ejected from two games in one day. "If you approach Billy Martin right, he's okay," former pitcher Ron Guidry once said. "I avoid him altogether."

That was solid advice, as former Twins pitcher Dave Boswell learned during Billy's year as a manager with Minnesota in 1969—Billy punched out Boswell and sent him to the hospital with twenty stitches. Martin wound up getting fired that autumn, no small accomplishment given that he guided Minnesota to the division title that year.

Billy was an excellent manager, no doubt about it. But his "Have You Got a Problem?" personality, his lack of respect for the people signing his paychecks and his friendship with Jack Daniel's and Jim Beam made him annually the Manager Most Likely to Be Found at Kinko's Copying His Resume.

The Tigers, Rangers and Athletics also fired Billy (he had this annoying habit of using pitchers until their arms resembled linguini), but Steinbrenner and the Yankees were his personal pink slip. You know how Krispy Kreme has the "Hot Donuts" red light that they turn on when the donuts are hot out of the oven? The Yankees should have had one for Billy that flashed "Fired/Not Fired."

Steinbrenner fired him for the first time in 1978 (after he said of Reggie and the Boss, "The two of them deserve each other. One's a born liar and the other's convicted"), and again in 1979 (after he beat up a marshmallow salesman in a Minnesota bar—class, pure class). He also fired him in 1983. And in 1985. And in 1988 (shortly after he got in a fight at a Texas strip bar—dignity, always dignity). Steinbrenner no doubt would have hired and fired him again had it not been for the difficulty of exhuming the body after Billy was killed in a car wreck in 1989.

2. Joe DiMaggio, outfielder (1936–51)

Mr. Coffee lived the richest life of anyone who wasn't a Beatle. He not only played center field for a perennial World Series team in the country's largest city, he followed up his baseball career by marrying Marilyn Monroe. That's like winning the lottery and having Halle Berry bring the weekly payments to your door. As if that wasn't enough, Hemingway, Rodgers and Hammerstein, and Paul Simon and Art Garfunkel evoked Mr. Coffee's name in their works, with Simon and Garfunkel memorializing him in the hit song "Mrs. Robinson."

Where have you gone, Joe DiMaggio?
A nation turns its lonely eyes to you
Woo, woo, woo

People always assume Simon and Garfunkel referred to Mr. Coffee out of profound reverence, but Simon once told Mickey Mantle that it was all about syllables and rhythm. Apparently, Moose Skowron just wasn't long enough a name. Simon meant more than that, of course, not that Mr. Coffee cared. When the song first came out, he wanted to sue Simon.

Typical. That's the thing with Mr. Coffee. He always carefully protected his image to give the impression he was classy, dignified and above the rabble, when in reality he was just a stingy old man.

According to Pulitzer Prize winner Richard Ben Cramer's biography *Joe DiMaggio: The Hero's Life*, Mr. Coffee beat Marilyn and had mob connections. He also was so tight with his money that he occasionally walked to the laundromat to save fifteen cents a load and even refused to sign baseballs for the hospital that bore his name, forcing the Joe DiMaggio Children's Hospital to buy his autograph on the open market if it wanted any for fund-raisers.

And the open market commanded the sort of prices rarely seen outside a Halliburton price catalogue—Mr. Coffee demanded a minimum of $150 an autograph at one point. And even at $150, there were so many restrictions, the NCAA would consider it overkill. For instance, when Mr. Coffee appeared at a "Yankees Legends" signing in 1995, Cramer reported in his book, large notices were posted that read:

RULES AND REGULATIONS FOR AUTOGRAPHS.

Joe will not sign the following: Bats, jerseys, Perez-Steele cards, baseball cards, plates, multi-signature balls, original art, statues, lithos, gloves, albums, caps, wool or cloth items, flats over 16X20, books, items not related to baseball, photos or (National League) baseballs, equipment or personalizations.

Sure, that narrowed the possibilities a bit, but at least Mr. Coffee didn't rule out *absolutely everything*. For example, there was no mention of watermelons.

And at least the sign let you know where you stood. If Mr. Coffee didn't rule it out on his list, you knew it was acceptable.

Except that the fine print also noted that "Joe has the right to refuse any item that in his opinion fits into these categories."

What the hell is this? A @$%#ing watermelon? Vinnie, take this punk out into the alley and teach him a lesson.

Hmmm. Well, maybe you still could slip something in, like the chipped Louisville Slugger your father had been saving since Bat Day at Yankee Stadium in 1940, just on the off chance that Mr. Coffee would be in a good mood and sympathize with a lifelong Yankees fan.

"PLEASE DO NOT BRING UP ANY ITEMS THAT JOE WILL NOT SIGN."

Aw, hell. What do you say we forget it and get in the Mickey Rivers line?

Still. A lot of guys who were products of the Depression were tightwads. Heck, Ted Williams occasionally would pay by check on the assumption that people would rather keep his signature as a souvenir than send it to the bank (and let's not even discuss the bickering kids and the whole frozen head thing). What really was annoying about DiMaggio was his insistence on being introduced as "The Greatest Living Ballplayer," as if Willie Mays and Hank Aaron were pushing up daisies, or worse, had never been born. That's like claiming you're the world's strangest man while standing in the same room as Michael Jackson and David Gest.

Not even death put an end to this arrogance. After he died, the city of San Francisco wanted to honor Mr. Coffee by naming a park in his old North Beach neighborhood after him, but his lawyer, Morris Engleberg, filed a suit to prevent that honor because he didn't think the park was good enough to bear the DiMaggio name.

We can only assume that to be considered adequate for Mr. Coffee, the park needed a grove of Redwoods, purple mountains, a ski lodge, a two-hundred-foot waterfall, a couple geysers, bighorn sheep and buffalo roaming among the antelope.

And, naturally, a park ranger charging $15 per car admission.

Where have you gone, Joe DiMaggio?
Mr. Rawlings turns his sweet spot for you to sign
Ka-ching, ka-ching, ka-ching
What's that you say, Morris Engleberg?
Joltin' Joe is charging $350 a ball?
Whoah, ohhh, ohhh.

3. Reggie Jackson, outfielder/DH (1977–81)

There are two man-made items visible from outer space: the Great Wall of China and Reggie's ego.

This, after all, is a man who authored two autobiographies by age thirty-eight, both titled *Reggie*. "I am the best in baseball," he wrote in the first *Reggie*. "That may sound conceited but I want to be honest about how I feel."

Thanks for the honesty, Reggie. And mind you, that was published in 1975, when he hit .253 and struck out 133 times. And he hadn't even played a single season in New York yet.

While still with the Athletics, Reggie famously told reporters that if he played in New York, "They would name a candy bar after me." Sure enough, they did. And in one of the greatest quotes in baseball history, Catfish Hunter said, "When you unwrap a Reggie bar, it tells you how good it is."

By the time Reggie finished his career, he had described himself as "the straw that stirs the drink" (see accompanying box); talked about "the magnitude of me"; said that, "The only reason I don't like playing in the World Series is I can't watch myself play"; and declared that "After Jackie Robinson, the most important black in baseball history is Reggie Jackson. I really mean that."

(Aaron, Mays and Curt Flood could not be reached for comment.)

"Reggie doesn't usually talk much with the other players, anyway," Sparky Lyle wrote in *The Bronx Zoo*. "Mostly, it's with the press. We get to read the bull he says in the paper the next day."

What was the true magnitude of Reggie? He did hit 563 home runs, sixth all-time when he retired; drove in 1,702 runs; won the 1973 MVP; hit all those World Series home runs; and reached the Hall of Fame his first year of eligibility. But he also holds the record for career strikeouts—2,597, nearly 400 more than the number-two whiffer and the equivalent of roughly five entire seasons of doing nothing but stepping up to the plate and swinging and missing. He finished with a .262 career average, which is lower than Raul Ibañez's.

He also was a terrible fielder, or as Billy put it, "It's not that Reggie is a bad outfielder. He just has trouble judging the ball and picking it up."

True, Reggie was Mr. October, but even that title is suspect. More accurately, he was Mr. October 12–19.

While he performed superbly in the World Series—he played in five series, won four championship rings and hit .357 with ten home runs (three in the final game of the 1977 series) and 24 RBIs in twenty-seven games—he played considerably poorer in the playoffs. In eleven league championship series, Reggie batted .227 with 20 RBIs in forty-five games, failing to reach the Mendoza line six times and falling short of his self-proclaimed 160 IQ four times. His team lost the ALCS almost as often as it won. Even in his celebrated 1977 postseason, he was benched for the final game of the playoffs after going 1 for 16 in the previous four.

In a typical case of Yankees propaganda, Reggie wears a Yankee cap on his Hall of Fame plaque, even though less than a quarter of his at-bats were with New York, he played more postseasons in Oakland than in New York, and he began and finished his career with the Athletics. (Steinbrenner is believed to have paid for the cap by giving Reggie a front-office job.)

Fittingly though, his mouth is open on the plaque.

  Mr. October Explains How to Stir a Drink

"You know, this team . . . it all flows from me. I've got to keep it going. I'm the straw that stirs the drink."
—Reggie, as quoted in *Sport* magazine, June 1977

"You wouldn't think it would take someone with an IQ of 160 to demonstrate proper bartending techniques to a major league team, but you'd be surprised at how poorly the Yankees stirred their drinks before I showed up.

"Now, take Chris Chambliss. Good hitter, nice man. But he always preferred a swizzle stick, as if that was going to do him any good. Could he sip his drink with a swizzle stick and see if he had stirred it enough? Hell, no, you need a straw for that. After I showed him the technique I developed while leading Oakland to three consecutive World Series, he picked right up on it. But it just makes you wonder where he would be had I not been there to share my wisdom. Fifth place, probably.

"But at least Chambliss used a swizzle stick. Thurman Munson used to dunk his index finger right into his Bacardi and Coke and give it a little swirl, can you believe that? He would even do it when he bought a round for you and then hand over the drink as if he had never heard the word hepatitis, which he probably hadn't, the big ignoramus. He certainly couldn't spell it. And trust me, he wasn't too careful about washing his hands, either. I tried explaining patiently how many germs were on the average New Yorker's finger, but there was no talking to him. Munson always knew best. Thickest skull of any teammate I ever played with. And dirty? International Harvester couldn't clear all the dirt under his fingernails.

"Then there was Mickey Rivers. He always ordered his drinks with those little tropical umbrellas in them. You can't stir a drink with one of those—they aren't long enough. But Mick didn't care. I attempted to show him how to stir with a straw and the next thing you know, he's using it to shoot spit wads across the bar at Lou Piniella. And pretty soon Willie Randolph and Bucky Dent are shooting back and they're all laughing as if it's some big Neil Simon comedy. No wonder the Yankees got swept by Cincinnati the year before I showed up.

"I don't blame them, though. Stirring drinks simply wasn't covered in the Yankees' fundamental drills each spring. Which is no surprise. Billy never mixed a drink in his life—he drank straight out of the bottle.

"A player of lesser character and weaker resolve would have left it at that, but I went to Steinbrenner's office the second week of the season to convey the extent of the problem. He nodded his head and assured me he would take care of it. And sure enough, the next day we receive a dozen cases of straws in the clubhouse. Only they were paper straws! Can you imagine? You can't stir a drink properly with a paper straw! It's too flimsy to handle the ice cubes and it falls apart before you're even half finished with your drink. That's typical Steinbrenner, though. He always went cheap on the little items. He could never see the bigger picture even when I laid it out for him.

"Anyway, to make a long story short, I eventually taught the Yankees how to stir their drinks and I hit five home runs in the World Series that fall, including three in Game 6—on three consecutive swings, a feat that had never been accomplished before and I dare say never will again—and then I showed everyone how to open a champagne bottle without making the cork pop and pour the champagne over their heads and still give the TV cameras a solid sound bite. I led the Yankees to the World Series again the next year and in 1981, too. But then Steinbrenner got cheap again when my contract came up, so I took my considerable talents to the Angels, where they were appreciated. We went to the postseason that very autumn while the Yankees dynasty dissolved immediately.

"While my departure was the overwhelming reason behind the Yankees' decline, there was another factor. I hate to disparage another player, but, well . . . Dave Winfield had some very strange ideas about mixed drinks."

4. David Wells, pitcher (1997–98, 2002–03)

Dean Vernon Wormer says in *Animal House* that "being fat, drunk and stupid is no way to go through life," but that policy worked well enough for Boomer during much of his career. He is the man fast-food marketers must have had in mind when they coined the term "Biggie-size."

Pitching with his jersey unbuttoned and untucked, Wells was such a defiant slob that he made sportswriters look slim and fashionable. The day before what would become his final start as a Yankee in the 2003 World Series, the Boomer told reporters that his career "goes to show you don't need to bust your ass every day to be successful."

No kidding. Wells was so poorly conditioned that he once missed part of spring training due to gout. No, really. Gout.

Being fat is certainly no crime, and in fact it often makes professional athletes that much more appealing to fans, who can readily identify with them (I'm thinking Tony Gwynn and John Kruk here). But that wasn't the case with Wells, who kept the Hell from his "Hells Angels" upbringing. He challenged Billy's club record for most drunken brawls, broke his hand in a 1997 fight and bragged that he was half drunk when he pitched his famous perfect game (though the ever-optimistic Yankees preferred to view him as being half sober).

"As of this writing, fifteen men in the history of organized baseball have ever thrown a perfect game. Only *one* of those men did it half drunk, with bloodshot eyes, monster breath and a raging, skull-rattling hangover. That would be me. Never in the history of professional sports has a feat so difficult been accomplished by an athlete so *thoroughly* shot."

That quote, of course, is from Wells's 2003 memoir, *Perfect I'm Not*, the most accurately titled book since Anne Heche's *Call Me Crazy*. The book's release infuriated club management, in part because the Yankees infuriate easily when anyone challenges their image and because Wells overstated his accomplishment—after all, Mantle also performed some of his extraordinary feats while thoroughly shit-faced. Wells eventually was forced to apologize for proof-reading the book while wearing his beer goggles.

That Wells might backtrack a bit from what he "wrote" was no surprise given that he so often backed away from what he said. He made a verbal agreement to pitch with the Diamondbacks in 2002, then backed out of it and signed with the Yankees instead. Not that he played favorites. Wells also agreed to a deal with the Yankees after the 2003 season, then backed out of it and signed with the Padres instead.

Constantly pissing off someone (he brought disgraced O. J. Simpson detective Mark Fuhrman into the clubhouse one day), Wells changed teams eight times in his career, including seven times in a nine-year span.

Through it all, he remained stubbornly unapologetic for his poor conditioning. "I'll leave the workouts and conditioning to those guys," Wells said the night before starting Game 5 of the 2003 World Series. "They can write a book and do videos and they can make money on that. And I'll write the one how not to [work out], and we'll weigh the both of them."

The next night he lasted one inning before retreating to the Official Heineken Trainers Table with a sore back, leaving Torre and his teammates hung out to dry.

Somewhere, Dean Wormer was smiling.

5. Alex Rodriguez, third baseman (2004–)

For fans, the Curse of A-Rod is that the Yankees signed the league's best player and added him to their roster. For Rodriguez, the Curse of A-Rod is that teams seem to do better without him.

He left the Seattle Mariners after they had fallen two victories shy of the World Series in 2000, saying that his number-one priority heading into free agency was to sign with a contender. He then signed a $252 million contract with the last-place Rangers, a team that even the least knowledgeable of fans could see had insufficient pitching to raise them in the standings any time in the near future.

The Mariners set the American League record for victories their first season without Rodriquez while the Rangers finished in last place each of the three years A-Rod played there, finishing a combined ninety-nine games out of first place.

Frustrated with losing, A-Rod honored less than a third of the contract before saying that he wanted out.

First, he tried to arrange a trade to the Red Sox, but when that didn't work out he took responsibility as the Rangers team captain, told reporters that he felt "good about with who I am in bed with and who I am married to with the Rangers," looked forward to negotiating a new contract with the Rangers that would keep him in Texas "into my forties," that "I definitely think I'm going to be here for a long time" and that "I feel a grand responsiblity not only to the Texas Rangers but to our fans." He also delivered one of the classic quotes in sports history, saying, "I'm probably pretty sure it will work out for the best."

Three weeks later he helped arrange his trade to the Yankees.

A-Fraud to Texas Fans: Go to Hell!

If his commitment to Texas sounded a little hollow, it wasn't surprising. He may be one of the game's greatest players, but A-Rod also is the Eddie Haskell of baseball, always saying what he thinks will sound good instead of expressing sincere emotion.

Without Rodriguez, the Rangers improved dramatically, won eighty-nine games and nearly made the playoffs. As for A-Rod and the Yankees? Well, when "Mr. October" was a mere victory away from reaching the World Series in 2004, he had one hit and no RBIs in his final 15 at-bats while the Yankees choked away their 3–0 lead and failed to reach the World Series for just the second time in seven years.

Granted, slumps happen to everyone, often at awkward times, and Rodriguez was hardly the only Yankee to struggle late in that series. He was, however, the only Yankee to embarrass himself with a play so bush league he should have been forced to ride his bicycle home without a snow cone. After hitting a weak roller in the eighth inning of Game 6, A-Rod reached out and slapped the ball out of Bronson Arroyo's glove when the pitcher tried to tag him. Umpires called him out for interference, and the Yankees never threatened again in the series.

"It was a classless play. Unprofessional," Boston first baseman Kevin Millar said after the game. "That's just as unprofessional as you're going to see. Play the game hard and play the game right. He's got to brush his teeth looking in the mirror, not with his head down."

So, in the end, A-Rod was right at the winter press conference. He was probably pretty sure it was going to work out for the best, and it did. He and the Yankees lost.

What Was *He Thinking?*

The top ten things Alex Rodriguez might have been thinking when he slapped the ball out of Boston pitcher Bronson Arroyo's glove during the American League championship series:

10. "I wonder if there's an incentive bonus in my contract for being named the ALCS MVP."

9. "We really need to win tonight and wrap up this series—Barneys' annual autumn sale on handbags starts tomorrow."

8. "What's Bo Derek doing on the field?"

7. "Geez, another weak grounder? Maybe I should have borrowed Sheffield's steroid cream."

6. "What I like best about playing in the postseason is getting to meet all those cool celebrities from Fox's primetime shows."

5. "This is where I can finally carve my name into postseason history."

4. "I hope they get the plastic tarp hung over my locker good and tight—champagne would just ruin my new DKNY outfit."

3. "Does Derek really like me or does he just say he does to be nice?"

2. "Is it too late to demand a trade to the Red Sox?"

1. "Two hundred and forty-eight million, two hundred and forty-nine million, two hundred and fifty million . . ."

6. George Weiss, general manager (1936–60)

How bad was this guy? He made Steinbrenner look like Jimmy Carter.

Beginning in the Depression, Weiss organized New York's powerful farm system and officially became their general manager in 1948. With him in charge, New York won five consecutive World Series and ten of the next twelve American League pennants. The rest of his resume is not so glowing.

The Yankees were notoriously tight with salaries in those days, thanks in no small part to Weiss, a cold and humorless man the players detested. After the Yankees swept the Phillies in the 1950 World Series, David Halberstam writes in *Summer of '49*, Weiss got up at the team party and announced that because the series had lasted only four games, the owners had not made as much money as they should have, so salaries would have to be held down the following year. *Now, get back to your celebration, but just remember, boys, that's a no-host bar.* He hired private detectives to follow his players around so he could use their night-life indiscretions against them during contract negotiations.

In *The Mick*, Mantle details Weiss's negotiating style when the center fielder demanded a raise to $65,000 after winning the 1956 triple crown. After listening to Mantle's reasoning, Weiss icily pulled out a batch of reports from private detectives detailing his late-night carousing and said: "'I wouldn't want this to get into [your wife's] hands.'"

As despicable as that was, his record on black ballplayers was even worse. The Yankees didn't integrate until 1955 with Elston Howard, who remained the team's only African American in the regular lineup until after Weiss left the team. "I will never allow a black man to wear a Yankee uniform," Weiss declared once. "Boxholders from Westchester don't want that sort of crowd. They would be offended to have to sit with [blacks]." Only he didn't use the term "blacks."

Impressed by the championships and conveniently ignoring the rest of his record, Cooperstown enshrined Weiss in the Hall of Fame in 1971. In a delicious bit of irony, he was inducted the same day as Satchel Paige, a man he didn't feel was of major league caliber because of his skin color. Their two plaques are mounted together, one above and one below.

It's unfortunate a great man like Satchel has to spend his days with that sort of crowd.

7. Darryl Strawberry, outfielder/DH (1995–99)

Once asked whether Strawberry was a dog, Tommy Lasorda shook his head. "He is not a dog; a dog is loyal and runs after balls."

Has anyone ever overcome so much (a childhood in the Crenshaw area of Los Angeles followed by cancer in adulthood) and still squandered away so much money, talent and potential to so thoroughly mess up their lives? Outside of *Nip/Tuck*, that is?

There is a certain tragedy to Strawberry's story and it's easy to feel sorry for his troubles with drug addiction. But his violent temper and disrespect for women are disturbing.

Strawberry broke his wife's nose in 1986, was accused of domestic assault in 1993 and beat up his girlfriend. He was suspended three times for substance abuse and spent so much time in rehab there should be a wing named after him at the Betty Ford Clinic. He's been prosecuted for tax evasion and has failed to make child support payments. He's been kicked out of rehab for having sex with another patient and jailed for violating curfew.

Naturally, he also co-wrote a self-help book, *Recovering Life*. The book came out a couple months after he had been arrested for soliciting sex from an undercover cop and possessing cocaine, and about a year before being arrested for violating parole during a hit-and-run while driving under the influence. The book had probably reached the remainders table by the time Strawberry was thrown in jail for eleven months for violating parole for the sixth time.

And shortly after Strawberry was released from jail in 2003, the Yankees hired him as an instructor for player development. "He is a true professional with, I believe, the ability to be a great teacher," Steinbrenner said in a statement just before placing a large "Kick Me" sign on his own back.

Alas, Strawberry quit a couple weeks into spring training, depriving aspiring Yankees prospects from learning the proper fundamentals for filing their income taxes, snorting a line of cocaine and picking up a prostitute.

8. Paul O'Neill, right fielder (1993–2001)

The Proper Care and Feeding of Paul O'Neill

1. Make certain the batting helmet fits snugly on the outfielder's head before allowing him to bat. This will not prevent O'Neill from throwing the helmet but it will delay him long enough for his teammates to seek cover.

2. Speak softly and lovingly to him, saying reassuring things, such as "You're right, darling, that pitch was a foot outside" and "There, there, snookums—Daddy going to go and get a new umpire for you."

3. Don't raise your hand or your voice when scolding but be firm nonetheless. Say, "You can't go out and play in right field until you put down the water cooler."

4. Do not give O'Neill objects with a sharp edge or anything that could get lodged in the throat. He will only throw them on the field.

5. While breast-feeding is a matter of personal preference once rosters expand in September, do not under any circumstance let David Wells bottle-feed him.

O'Neill batted .288 in his career, hit 281 home runs, drove in 1,269 runs and won five world championship rings (one with Cincinnati). He also splintered 316 bats, shattered sixty-seven batting helmets and destroyed eighteen water coolers. Those are unofficial, conservative estimates, naturally. The exact figures are probably much higher.

Was there a bigger crybaby in the game than O'Neill? He struck out 1,166 times, which is amazing given that, based on the withering stares he gave home plate umpires, pitchers never threw him a strike in his entire career. An umpire would call strike three on O'Neill and the next thing you know so much debris was being thrown by the Yankees dugout it was as if Chuck Knoblauch had tried to complete a double play.

Yankees fans always defend O'Neill by saying that his temper only showed how much he cared about the game and that he was only expressing anger at his own failures. Yeah, right—and Johnny Depp tears up hotel suites because it shows he's still upset about his performance in *The Astronaut's Wife*. Saying O'Neill's tantrums are a sign of his intense passion is the same thing as saying that all the other players don't care at all because they return to the dugout calmly and maturely. Plus, if O'Neill's anger was self-directed, then how come so many home plate umpires are still wiping the spittle off their faces years after his last game?

At least O'Neill's career provided comic diversion in John Irving's novel *The Fourth Hand*. The novel's protagonist, Patrick Wallingford, is repeatedly mistaken for O'Neill by his New York City doorman. What makes the doorman's confusion so odd is that he continues to make the mistake even after a lion bites off Wallingford's left hand.

"Don't worry, Mr. O'Neill," the doorman told Patrick. "The things they can do in rehab today . . . well, you wouldn't believe. It's too bad it wasn't your right hand—you bein' a leftie is gonna make it tough— but they'll come up with somethin', I know they will."

Irving never fully explains why the doorman confuses Wallingford for O'Neill, but I suspect it was because Wallingford was in the habit of smashing the lobby water cooler with his umbrella.

9. Bucky Dent, shortstop (1977–82)

It isn't so much that the mere mention of Dent's name causes Bostonians to speak in tongues and shake as uncontrollably as a Katharine Hepburn bobblehead doll—hell, Dent was just doing his job when he hit his 1978 game-deciding home run over the Green Monster.

No, what's infuriating about Russell Earl Dent is the way he, like all true Yankees, can never let anyone forget the moment. To forever remind fans of one of the darkest days in baseball history, Dent even built a replica of the Green Monster at his hitting school in Florida. And before Game 7 of the 2004 ALCS against the Red Sox, he threw out the first pitch. What's next, Mr. Sensitive, building a replica of Wrigley Field with an animatronic Steve Bartman dropping foul balls in the stands?

By the way, the rest of Dent's career wasn't quite as dramatic as that one afternoon in Boston. He played twelve years, never hit more than eight home runs in a season, retired with a .247 average, and the only category in which he ever led the league was sacrifice bunts. He also was one of the worst managers in Yankees history, guiding New York to a 36-53 record over two seasons. He was so bad that the Yankees chose to replace him with Stump Merrill. That's like the U.S. attorney general being replaced by Barney Fife.

So give it a rest, Bucky. After all, do the Red Sox show your performance in *The Dallas Cowboys Cheerleaders* TV movie on their video board?

10. Roger Clemens, pitcher (1999–2003)

In his book *Where the Spirits Dwell*, writer Tobias Schneebaum ventures into the most remote areas of New Guinea to live among the native headhunters. These cannibals are said to cut off the limbs of their victims, eat their hearts to release their spirit and use their skulls as pillows. It's a remarkable tale but Schneebaum really didn't need to go to all that trouble.

He could have just gone to Yankee Stadium, where he would have found the world's most notorious headhunter standing on the mound and wearing number 22.

Remember how offended New York got in the 2003 playoffs with Boston when Pedro Martinez dared to throw a pitch at one of the great, esteemed Yankees and then motioned that he was prepared to hit another? The Yankees reaction to Pedro was a bit like Michael Jackson accusing sister Janet of embarrassing the family with her little Super Bowl performance. Because standing right in the Yankees dugout was the pitcher who treated every batter as his private video game—Clemens.

Clemens is one of the greatest pitchers in baseball history, but he also can be such a psycho that he once wore war paint to the mound for a must-win playoff game, then got himself ejected in the second inning. His most infamous performance, however, was during Game 2 of the 2000 World Series. That game was the first meeting between Clemens and Mike Piazza since the regular season, when the Rocket hit the Mets catcher so hard in the head with a fastball that Piazza's descendants will have to take Tylenol for most of their lives.

Thus, when the two met again in the World Series, all of New York and much of the nation leaned in to watch, anxiously wondering what would happen. Would Clemens bean him again? Would Piazza take him deep? Would the two shake hands, stop the game and offer a road map toward peace in the Middle East?

As it turned out, what happened wasn't nearly so predictable. Instead, Piazza shattered his bat hitting a ground ball and Clemens grabbed its splintered business end and angrily hurled it toward Piazza as he ran toward first base. It was the most outlandish act ever committed on a baseball field that didn't involve a baseball made of flubber.

Completely bewildered by the attack, Piazza initiated the following exchange with Clemens:

Piazza: "Didst thou fling the remains of my severed batting instrument in my direction with malicious intent? Didst thou wish to cause injury to my person? Hast thou a complaint with my manner? What hast I done to offend thee? Pray, what say thou in this matter?"

Clemens: "RED-RUM!!! RED-RUM!!! RED-RUM!!! RED-RUM!!!"

The *New York Post* published a full-page photo of Clemens rearing back to hurl the bat at Piazza with the headline everyone was asking: "IS HE NUTS?"

Well, is he? Or just misunderstood?

On the one hand, Clemens pitched thirteen often spectacular seasons with the Red Sox, twice striking out twenty batters in a game and more importantly leading Boston to four division titles over the Yankees.

On the other hand, he also helped orchestrate a trade to the Yankees (this would have been like Giuliani running for mayor of Kabul on the Taliban ticket) and helped them to two more world championships. He so embraced Yankees culture that it was his ritual to rub the Ruth plaque prior to his starts. He also told Cooperstown that if they didn't have him wearing a New York logo on his Hall of Fame plaque he wouldn't show up for his induction ceremony.

Then again, he screwed the Yankees over by repeatedly maintaining that he was going to retire after the 2003 season, then changing his mind during the winter and signing with the Astros.

So, overall, it's probably a wash.

Honorable Mention

Steve Howe, pitcher (1991–96): Howe was already a six-time loser in 1991 when New York decided he would fit right in with the great tradition of Yankees drunks. And he was arrested for buying cocaine the very next season. Commissioner Fay Vincent banned him from baseball for life, making Howe the first player to receive a permanent ban for substance abuse, but an arbitrator overturned the suspension a few months later when the pitcher claimed he needed the drug to help him with his Attention Deficit Disorder. The Yankees, naturally, quickly re-signed him. Complained Vincent: "It's like saying you've had seven chances, but eight is the right number."

Don Zimmer, bench coach (1996–2003). The man Bill Lee christened "the Gerbil," Zimmer once accepted money to endorse Popeyes Fried Chicken and the NutriSystem weight-loss system—at the same time. That's the sort of thing that gained Zimmer a reputation as one of baseball's loveable characters, but he isn't. Upset that he wasn't being consulted when he was bench coach for Don Baylor with the Colorado Rockies in 1995, he got off the bench in the fifth inning of a game and quit. He called it a retirement, but less than a year later he was sitting on the Yankees bench next to Torre, with his unmistakable mug appearing on TV more often than *Law & Order* reruns. He earned his spot in Yankees infamy and on this list, however, during Game 3 of the 2003 playoff series with the Red Sox. Angered that Martinez had dared to hit a Yankee, he left the bench and charged across the field as if the Red Sox dugout was offering a Senior Citizen's Early Bird Special, cocking his arm to smack Pedro in the head. Placed in a no-win situation—if he let Zimmer hit him, he could be severely hurt, but if he defended himself he would be beating up a senior citizen—Martinez did about the only thing he could. He gripped Zimmer by the head (how could he avoid doing so with a melon like that?) and shoved him to the ground, producing this classic postgame quote from Clemens: "Andy Pettitte and I went over there and I saw a bald head on the ground. We weren't sure if it was Zim or David [Wells]."

Let's see. There's also reliever **Jeff Nelson**, who got into a fight with a Fenway Park bullpen worker/schoolteacher in 2003, and his henchman, **Karim Garcia**. And the moody **Chuck Knoblauch**, who once roughed up an autograph seeker in a hotel lobby and somehow missed a game due to frostbite in the middle of summer. And **Deion Sanders**, who had Reggie Jackson's ego and Ron Jackson's talent, and played with the Yankees just long enough to enrage White Sox catcher Carlton Fisk with his lack of hustle. And outfielder/bigot **Jake Powell**, one of the most miserable SOBs in the team's history. And first baseman/gambler **Hal Chase**. And **Joe Pepitone** and **Luis Polonia** and **Frank Crosetti** and **Kevin Brown** . . .

Awwww, don't get me started.

CHAPTER 5

The Ten Moments We Savor and the One We Savor the Most

The Yankees have won twenty-six world championships, thirty-nine pennants and forty-two overall titles. They've won more games than any other team and have sent seventeen players to Cooperstown wearing the NY logo on their caps. But it hasn't been all bad. Remember, they've lost the World Series more often than any other team as well.

Here are the ten greatest moments in Yankees history:

1. The Yankees blow a 3–0 lead—and the pennant—to the Red Sox (October 2004)

It was a greater reversal than if Ben Affleck had made a good movie. It was the most shocking collapse in U.S. history that did not involve Ken Lay, Enron and a federal investigation. And it brought more joy to more people than any previous sporting event, with the possible exception of when Brandi Chastain ripped off her jersey to reveal her sports bra.

Baseball played its one hundredth postseason in 2004 and in none of the previous ninety-nine had a team ever blown a 3–0 lead in a best-of-seven series. No team had ever even been forced to play a seventh game after taking a 3–0 lead and only one team had so much as been forced to play a sixth game. The Yankees themselves had won fifty-two postseason series, closing out opponent after opponent as coldly and calculatingly as a bank foreclosing on a farmer.

So when the Yankees embarrassed the Red Sox 19–8 in Game 3 to take their 3–0 lead and then had Mariano Rivera on the mound with a ninth inning lead in Game 4, the only solution left for fans was to drink themselves into a coma that would last until the end of the World Series.

But that's when the most succcessful team in postseason history inexplicably started playing so badly it was as if Walter Matthau was the manager.

With the World Series so close you could smell the champagne (or was that just the smell of the empties left over from David Wells?), the Yankees got beat in consecutive games on game-winning hits by David Ortiz, a player the Twins had released. They got beat by Curt Schilling, who took the mound with a bloody sock from an ankle injured so badly it required surgery. They lost to Derek Lowe pitching on two days' rest. And in the end, the Yankees lost four games in a row to complete an unprecedented, humiliating, reputation-deflating, fan-stunning, owner-panicking postseason collapse.

Of course, it isn't easy to play baseball when you have both hands wrapped around your throat.

At least, the sensitive New York media were understanding about the collapse, realizing that the most important thing was not the way the Yankees lost in the end but that they simply had played well enough for a while to even come so close. "THE CHOKE'S ON US," screamed the *Daily News*. "DAMNED YANKEES," griped the *New York Post*. David Letterman brought on Schilling to read the top ten secrets behind the collapse, including, "Number ten. Unlike the first three games, we didn't leave early to beat the traffic."

How to Be a Good Loser

The Yankees have so seldom faced adversity that their fans were at a loss when the team choked during the 2004 championship series. Here then is a short primer for Yankees fans about how to behave after a painful postseason.

1. Don't worry, Mr. Blackwell does not consider it a fashion faux pas if you can't buy a new championship T-shirt every single year. This may be difficult to believe but you can actually wear an old one for several seasons. In fact, some fans in Pittsburgh are still making do with ragged, faded yellow "We Are Family" T-shirts, which fortunately have come back into style, unlike the Pirates.

2. True, you'll have to get rid of all your "1918" T-shirts. But that's all right because you'll need the extra closet space for your "Schilling Sucks!" T-shirts.

3. After an embarrassing postseason finish, proper etiquette dictates that you act humble for a while, at least until playoff tickets go on sale. Until then, when you're taunting an opponent, it's "Mister Asshole!"

4. Don't set yourself up for unpleasant encounters with old rivals now suddenly eager for payback. For the time being, limit "Who's Your Daddy?" chants to safe opponents, such as the Tampa Bay Devil Rays and pitcher Dewon Brazelton.

5. Upgrade your cell phone plan for more unlimited minutes. You'll need them for the extra calls to WFAN to bitch about the team.

6. It's all right to feel bad about your team's poor finish but be sensitive of the feelings of other fans. When commiserating with Cubs fans, avoid such comments as "Can you imagine what it's like to go more than one year without being in the World Series?"

7. Curse Steinbrenner frequently.

And finally . . .

8. When Boston fans viciously taunt you, simply react in the same, mature way they did to all your taunts the past eighty years. Throw your cup of beer in their face and give them the finger.

2. Steinbrenner is banned for life
(July 31, 1990)

There are moments so dramatic and uplifting that the world stops spinning on its axis. The Allies liberate Paris. German youths tear down the Berlin Wall. And Commissioner Fay Vincent bans Steinbrenner from baseball for life.

I detail the reasons behind Steinbrenner's ban, the second of his career, in chapter 3, so I won't repeat them here other than to say they were for his role in paying Howard Spira to spy on Dave Winfield. In announcing the ban, Vincent said that he was able to "evaluate a pattern of behavior that borders on the bizarre" and that "Mr. Steinbrenner will have no further involvement in the management of the New York Yankees."

When fans at Yankee Stadium heard the news of the banishment, they responded with one voice at the outrageous exile of their beloved leader, chanting a deafening "George Must Go! George Must Go! George Must Go!"

During the 943 Days of George Held Hostage, the Yankees went a sublime 174-211 and finished in last place for the fourth time in club history; and just to prove that some things don't change, they even fired a manager (not that George had anything to do with that decision, of course).

But just when you thought it was safe to go back into the ballpark, Vincent gave Steinbrenner a reprieve and lifted the ban in 1993, clearing his return from Elba.

And in case anyone didn't appreciate what Steinbrenner's return meant, in the weeks leading up to spring training, he walked around his home wearing a black robe with "The Boss Is Back" written across the back and mulled over flying a Marilyn Monroe look-alike onto the field in a helicopter. He eventually ditched the Marilyn plan as too over-the-top and simply went with an understated appearance on the cover of *Sports Illustrated* dressed as Napoleon and riding a white horse.

3. Luis Gonzalez's bloop single beats Yankees in World Series (November 4, 2001)

The Yankees had won three consecutive world championships, reached the postseason seven consecutive years and won eleven consecutive postseason series when the World Series rolled around in 2001. They were such a regular presence that Steinbrenner undoubtedly wanted to charge other teams royalties for even playing in the same month.

Moreover, because of the September 11 terrorist attacks, the entire country had so rallied around New York that rooting against the Yankees, Seattle catcher Tom Lampkin said, "almost seems unpatriotic."

With the three consecutive world championships and the highest payroll in the game, people began talking about Yankees mystique and aura. And few doubted it when Jeter flew in from his Fortress of Solitude to rally them to victory against Oakland with his no-look shovel pass to nail Jeremy Giambi at the plate. Fewer still had doubts when Jeter homered off Byung-Hyun Kim to win Game 4 of the World Series. When things like that keep happening, you just assume the Yankees are always going to win in the end.

Heck, even Al-Jazeera picked the Yankees to beat the Diamondbacks in five.

Fortunately for baseball, Curt Schilling disagreed, saying Mystique and Aura sounded more like dancers in a strip club. He and Randy Johnson beat the Yankees in Games 1, 2 and 6 and then both went to the mound in Game 7 in the greatest teaming since Lennon and McCartney collaborated on *Abbey Road*.

Even so, the Yankees still were three outs from winning their fourth consecutive World Series, with closer Mariano Rivera on the mound. And then Rivera made a throwing error. And then Tony Womack drove in the tying run. And then Gonzalez dumped a bloop single over New York's drawn-in infield. The ball sailed beyond the range of Jeter, who evidently was exhausted from saving Metropolis from General Zod earlier in the day.

And just like that the Yankees' tyrannical reign was over. The Diamondbacks stormed the field, the Yankees walked silently to their clubhouse and Steinbrenner instructed someone to fire Costanza.

4. Josh Beckett shuts out the Yankees to win the World Series (October 25, 2003)

New York fans like to think of Yankee Stadium as sacred ground, like the fields of Gettysburg, the beaches of Normandy or the eighteenth fairway at Augusta. They revere it as such a cathedral that you would think it was the House That Brunelleschi Built, not Ruth. It's a wonder visiting teams aren't told to remove their caps and spikes and keep infield chatter to a minimum before taking the field.

That's why it was so satisfying to see the Marlins turn Yankee Stadium's field into their own private Woodstock following their 2003 World Series upset.

The Yankees were appearing in the World Series for the thirty-ninth time and in the postseason for the ninth consecutive fall, while the Marlins had never even finished in first place. So you could tell the Yankees took the Marlins a little lightly when Jeter started snoring during the national anthem before Game 1. By the time the Yankees realized they were in trouble—about the same instant Florida shortstop Alex Gonzalez's home run sailed over the left-field wall to win Game 4—it was too late. Gonzalez's home run evened the series, the Marlins took the lead by winning Game 5 and then sent Josh Beckett to the mound for the clincher in Game 6.

The return to Yankee Stadium was supposed to wake up New York like the smell of roasted chestnuts on an autumn morning, but the lineup remained as sluggish and inefficient as the workers in the concession stands. Pitching on three days' rest, Beckett completely shut down the vaunted Yankees offense on five hits. Just twenty-three, Beckett became the first postseason pitcher since Warren Spahn to shut out New York in Yankee Stadium. With just seventeen victories for the back of his baseball card and a .500 career record, he became the first pitcher to shut out the Yankees in a World Series clincher since Lew Burdette did it in 1957.

Evidently, Mystique and Aura called in sick that night.

When Beckett tagged out Jorge Posada for the final out, the stunned Yankees fans couldn't have been more silent if Steinbrenner had just announced the next season's ticket prices. The Yankees had been whipped by a team with a guy in a fish head for a mascot and with a payroll that was $110 million less than New York's.

As Steinbrenner crawled aboard his sedan chair for the long ride home ("I told Cashman we should have spent more money!"), the Marlins swarmed his field for the wildest party ever held in a ballpark that didn't involve dynamiting a mountain of disco records. Players and families danced around the field, pulling up grass for souvenirs while pouring down bottles of booze. Beckett stood at home plate and chugged a thirty-two-ounce bottle of beer. Gonzalez stretched out on the grass behind his shortstop position and savored a bottle of champagne. So many players swarmed Monument Park it looked like Yellowstone in peak season.

Hey, we're almost out of booze. Could someone run to the Yankees clubhouse and grab another keg from Wells's locker?

5. Steinbrenner beaten up in elevator
(October 25, 1981)

Yes, the Yankees reached the World Series in 1981, a happening that normally causes as much autumn dread as the debut of another TV series with Tom Greene. But instead, this series was as welcome as anything David E. Kelley, Stephen Bochco or Aaron Sorkin ever brought to a cathode ray tube.

First there was Winfield's struggle. Less than a year after Steinbrenner made him the highest-paid player in American sports history, Winfield went 1 for 22, and his slump was so deep that when he finally singled for his lone hit in Game 5, he asked for the baseball.

Midway through the series New York traded outfield prospect Willie McGee to the Cardinals for pitcher Bob Sykes, one of the most lopsided deals in major league history. McGee went on to become one of the best players in baseball, while injuries prevented Sykes from ever pitching in the majors again.

New York won the first two games at home, then lost the next four (including Game 4, when Reggie dropped a fly ball and New York blew a three-run lead) to become the sixth Yankees team to lose the final game of the World Series at the stadium. "I want to sincerely apologize to the people of New York and to the fans of the New York Yankees everywhere for the performance of the Yankees team in the World Series," Steinbrenner insensitively announced in a press release after the game. "I also want to assure you that we will be at work immediately to prepare for 'eighty-two."

The Yankees would not reach the postseason again for fourteen years, by which point McGee had almost two thousand hits, two batting titles, three gold gloves, an MVP award and had played in four World Series and four All-Star games.

The sweetest moment of the series, however, occurred after Game 5 in Los Angeles, when Steinbrenner mysteriously broke his hand. While many suspected that he broke the hand by punching a wall in anger, Steinbrenner claimed that he broke it in a fight in the hotel elevator with two Dodgers fans who had rudely called the Yankees a bunch of chokers and hit him over the head with a bottle. "I clocked them," Steinbrenner boasted. "There are two guys in this town looking for their teeth and two guys who will probably sue me. . . . It's okay for me to criticize my players because I pay the checks and we're in this together. But when other people call them chokers, I've had enough."

Oddly, there were no witnesses to the fight and in the world's most litigious society, no one ever stepped forward to sue one of the most hated and controversial men in the country for assault. Then again, maybe they were just afraid Steinbrenner would give them even worse if they dared mess with him again.

The Elevator Gang Comes Clean

"A lot of people question whether Steinbrenner really got in a fight in the elevator in 1981 but I can assure you the story is true. I know—I'm still undergoing plastic surgery to repair the scars.

"The backstory to the fight is my friend Sam and I grew up in L.A., cleaning pools in high school for guys like Claude Osteen and Bill Singer and Willie Davis, so we were *huge* Dodger fans. By 1981 Sam was playing Biff Loman in an off-off-off-Broadway musical-comedy version of *Death of a Salesman* called *Everyone Loves Shaklee*, but he flew back for the series and was staying at the Yankees team hotel. It was great. We took turns calling Stein-brenner's room at three in the morning and asking him to explain the cost-of-living clause in Winfield's contract.

"Now, the same day the Dodgers won Game 5, my agent called and told me I had an audition at Paramount as the guy in *Officer and a Gentleman* who Louis Gossett Jr. yells at: 'Only two things come out of Oklahoma—steers and queers, and I don't see any horns on you, boy.' It was my big break, and to celebrate, Sam and I went down to Chateau Marmont, where we scored a couple lines from someone who swore he was friends with John Belushi's publicist's assistant's cousin. Then we drove over to Dodger Stadium for the game, where we had a beer for every out Winfield made the whole series.

"So, we were a little buzzed by the time we got back to the hotel. Not falling-down drunk like Nick Nolte on a Malibu highway or anything, more like Dudley Moore in *Arthur*. Anyway, we're in the elevator and guess who steps in. Yeah, Steinbrenner. And even though we can tell he is seriously pissed, Sam can't resist. So he says, 'Nice game, Mr. Steinbrenner,' and then grabs his throat like he's choking. And Steinbrenner says, 'I recognize that voice. You're the gentleman who keeps calling my hotel room.'

"Steinbrenner calmly took off his sport coat, removed his tie and stripped to his waist. And oh, my God, I know he doesn't look like it on TV, but that man is cut. He looked like Schwarzenegger before he met Maria and got off the steroids. And quick? I didn't even see the punches. One minute we're staring at the 'Momma Didn't Love Me' skull-and-rattlesnake tattoo on his chest and the next thing I know we're both lying on the floor with blood gushing from our mouths like we were in a Tarantino flick.

"Steinbrenner says, 'Clumsy me—I meant to push the button for my floor.' Then he puts his shirt back on, tosses a handful of hundreds on our bodies and says, 'This should cover your dental bills. But may I suggest that in the future you show a little more respect to the greatest team in American sports.' And then the elevator doors open and he gets off on his floor.

"So, that's the real story about the elevator fight. Sam wigged out after that and moved to Chanhassen, Minnesota, to clean pools and, like I said, I'm still going through plastic surgery for it. Well, not so much surgery—the scars were taken care of years ago—but I'm getting a little Botox work right now because you have to stay young in this town to have any chance at all and my agent says he thinks he can get me a part as a waiter on *The O.C.* if I can just pass for twenty-two."

6. Don Mattingly is benched for not getting a haircut (August 15, 1991)

The late 1980s and early 1990s were glorious days for baseball. Thanks in part to owners colluding to hold down salaries, small-market clubs were going from last place to world champs in a single year, Minnesota was setting attendance records and the biggest stars played for the Athletics, Twins, Reds, Rangers and Mariners.

And best of all, the Yankees were baseball's biggest punch line that didn't involve Madonna.

The most delicious moment was during the historic 1991 season. While both Minnesota and Atlanta were going from worst to first, the Yankees were humiliating themselves so much even the plaques in Monument Park were turning red with embarrassment.

They benched team captain Don Mattingly for not getting a haircut.

Yes, Donnie Baseball, the best and most popular player on the roster, the heart and soul of the Yankees, the 1984 batting champ and the 1985 MVP, was deemed unworthy of representing the team because his hair was too long. Manager Stump Merrill sent Steve Sax, Mel Hall, Matt Nokes and Kevin Maas onto the field that day but Mattingly had to sit on the bench in disgrace.

New York was eleven games under .500 and in fifth place, and clearly it was all Mattingly's fault for not going to the barber.

"I'm overwhelmed by the pettiness of it," Mattingly told reporters, saying that he was "kind of confused and surprised." He added that he had asked the Yankees to trade him (preferably to a team that wasn't so uptight about the length of their players' hair, such as the morally degenerate Twins).

The Yankees have a thing about hair. During the national anthem of his first game in his first season as owner in 1973, Steinbrenner wrote down the numbers of the players whose hair was too long and ordered them to have it cut. He also recalled the team yearbooks because too many players were pictured with long hair. He forced Thurman Munson to shave his beard in 1977 and ordered Reggie to shave during the 1980 playoffs. Oscar Gamble had to cut his celebrated Afro in 1976.

Are there any questions why this man donated money to Nixon?

Mattingly's benching lasted only one day before the club was embarrassed into putting the team captain back in the lineup. Mattingly even got his hair cut and auctioned off the clippings for charity.

So, Hairgate all worked out for the best. Everyone had a good laugh at the Yankees' expense and the affair produced a memorable exchange in the classic "Homer at the Bat" episode of *The Simpsons*, when Mr. Burns dumps Mattingly from his team of ringers for violating club grooming policy . . .

Mr. Burns: "Mattingly, I thought I told you to shave those sideburns, you hippie! Get off my team, you're fired!"

Mattingly: "Whatever (muttering to himself as he walks away) . . . still like him better than Steinbrenner."

7. Yankees trade Jay Buhner for Ken Phelps (July 21, 1988)

The bad thing about the Yankees is that they always fatten up in mid-season by trading some no-name prospect for a high-priced star who leads them to the World Series. The good thing is that sometimes these no-names wind up becoming stars themselves.

Of all the "rising prospects for fading veterans" deals made at the trade deadline, this was the most delicious.

Ken Phelps was a powerful left-handed DH for the Mariners, hitting ninety-eight home runs from 1984 to 1988 (though somehow driving in only 239 runs). Steinbrenner just had to have him, so he traded outfield prospect Jay Buhner to get him. Phelps, who was thirty-four at the time, hit eighteen home runs the rest of his career while Buhner hit 307 home runs, drove in 951 runs, won a gold glove and made the All-Star team in his thirteen seasons with the Mariners. He also reminded New York of what it gave up when he hit one of the longest home runs at Yankee Stadium in recent memory.

Best of all, though, the trade produced a classic moment on *Seinfeld* when Steinbrenner mistakenly tells the Constanzas that their son George is dead.

Estelle (crying): "*I can't believe it, he was so young. How could this have happened?*"

Steinbrenner: "*Well, he'd been logging some pretty heavy hours, first one in in the morning, last one to leave at night. That kid was a human dynamo.*"

Estelle: "*Are you sure you're talking about George?*"

Steinbrenner: "*You are Mr. and Mrs. Costanza?*"

Frank (yelling): "*What the hell did you trade Jay Buhner for?!? He had thirty home runs, over one hundred RBIs last year, he's got a rocket for an arm, you don't know what the hell you're doin'!!*"

Steinbrenner: "*Well, Buhner was a good prospect, no question about it. But my baseball people love Ken Phelps's bat. They kept saying 'Ken Phelps, Ken Phelps.'*"

8. New York's Andy Hawkins pitches a no-hitter— and loses (July 1, 1990)

Ah, 1990. The year inspires sly smiles on baseball fans the way 1966 inspires sighs from wine lovers. It was the year Stump Merrill— a man whose managerial style resembled Homer Simpson working on a Rubik's Cube—was allowed to write out lineup cards, the year the Yankees finished in last place for the first time in a quarter century, the year Yankees ace Tim Leary lost nineteen games and the year Vincent banned Steinbrenner from baseball for life.

Truly, the Yankees had sunk so low that Billy Martin could look them in the eye from his grave.

No one symbolized the Yankees' collapse better than Andy Hawkins, who went 5-12 with a 5.37 ERA in 1990. No one, not even a Yankee (okay, maybe a Yankee) deserved the misfortune Hawkins endured during two delicious weeks that July. On July 12, he was the losing pitcher when Melido Perez no-hit the Yankees. Six days earlier, he pitched eleven shutout innings against the Twins at Yankee Stadium—and lost when he gave up two runs in the twelfth inning.

And then there was July 1, the day that started it all.

In the most memorable game of his career and in one of the most memorable in the eighty-two-year history of old Comiskey Park, Hawkins took a no-hitter into the eighth inning against the White Sox. Unfortunately for Hawkins, the Yankees hadn't scored a run so the game was tied 0–0 when he retired the first two batters in the bottom of the eighth.

And then third baseman Mike Blowers bobbled Sammy Sosa's routine grounder for an error.

And then Hawkins walked Ozzie Guillen to put runners on first and second.

And then he walked Lance Johnson on four pitches to load the bases.

And then Robin Ventura hit a routine fly ball to left field . . . and Jim Leyritz dropped it. Three runs scored.

And then Ivan Calderon hit a fly ball to gold glover Jesse Barfield in right field . . . and Barfield dropped it. Ventura scored.

Dan Pasqua finally popped up to shortstop Alvaro Espinoza, who caught the ball. But the damage had been done. The White Sox had a 4–0 lead and the Yankees went quietly in the ninth to give Hawkins the loss despite pitching a no-hitter and one of the great box score lines in history: 8 IP, 0 H, 4 R, 0 ER, 5 BB, 3 K.

Complained Hawkins: "I can't even throw a no-hitter right."

The Hawkins Box Score

New York	ab	r	h	rbi	Chicago	ab	r	h	rbi
Kelly cf	4	0	0	0	Johnson cf	3	1	0	0
Sax 2b	4	0	0	0	Ventura 3b	4	1	0	0
Mattingly 1b	4	0	0	0	Calderon dh	3	0	0	0
Balboni dh	4	0	0	0	Pasqua lf	4	0	0	0
Tolleson pr	0	0	0	0	Kittle 1b	3	0	0	0
Barfield rf	4	0	1	0	Lyons 1b	0	0	0	0
Leyritz lf	3	0	1	0	Karkovice c	2	0	0	0
Blowers 3b	3	0	0	0	Fletcher 2b	2	0	0	0
Geren c	3	0	1	0	Sosa rf	3	1	0	0
Espinoza ss	2	0	1	0	Guillen ss	2	1	0	0
Totals	31	0	4	0	Totals	26	4	0	0

New York 000 000 000-0
Chicago   000 000 04x-4

E-Ventura (2), Blowers, Leyritz, Barfield. DP-Chicago. LOB-New York 5, Chicago 3. Sac-Espinoza. SB-Sosa.

New York	IP	H	R	ER	BB	K
Hawkins L, 1-5	8	0	4	0	5	3

Chicago	IP	H	R	ER	BB	K
Hibbard	7	4	0	0	0	1
Jones W, 10-1	1	0	0	0	0	1
Radinsky	1	0	0	0	0	0

PB-Geren. T-2:34. A-30,642.

9. The Pine Tar Game, July 24 and August 18, 1983

It took twenty-five days, two court orders, two protests and a notarized letter to complete but nothing better revealed the Yankees' arrogance, pettiness, sense of entitlement and general lack of humor than the infamous Pine Tar Game between the Yankees and the Royals.

With two out, one on and the Royals trailing the Yankees 4–3 in the top of the ninth inning at Yankee Stadium, George Brett homered into the right-field seats to give Kansas City an apparent 5–4 lead. Billy Martin, however, complained that Brett's bat violated the rules because his pine tar extended more than eighteen inches from the handle and that he should be called out. Mesmerized by the Brat's beady red eyes, the umpiring crew agreed, which ended the game and gave the Yankees the win. Brett, naturally, was a little upset. With his eyes bugging out like a Warners Bros. cartoon figure, he stormed out of the dugout and attacked the umpires, earning a quick ejection.

The Royals subsequently protested the pine tar decision and league president Lee MacPhail (the former Yankees president and son of former Yankees owner Larry MacPhail) wisely ruled that the bat provided Brett no advantage. Overruling the umpires, he said the home run would count and ordered the two teams to resume the game from that point on August 18.

A true sportsman, Steinbrenner responded to the ruling by saying, "I wouldn't want to be Lee MacPhail living in New York."

And because the Yankees are *the Yankees* and accustomed to getting their way, they went to court to have the game postponed. After all, what business did a team from Kansas City have getting in the way of a Yankees victory? Kicking and screaming and embarrassing themselves to the very end, they announced that they would charge full admission for the game's completion (which wound up taking twelve minutes), then filed for an injunction to stop the game from being resumed at all. They received the injunction the morning of the eighteenth. MacPhail and the league immediately appealed and a second judge overturned the injunction in the afternoon, ordering the teams to complete playing the game that evening.

Even then the Yankees refused to give in. Just as the game was to resume with two out in the ninth, Martin protested that Brett had missed first base, second base or third base during his home run trot nearly a month earlier. When the umpires ruled otherwise, Martin demanded to know how they could be sure when it had been, in fact, a different crew umpiring the original game. Fortunately, MacPhail had ingeniously anticipated just such a ploy from the Brat and had gotten the original crew to sign a notarized affidavit that Brett had touched each base properly.

Still not satisfied, Billy argued until the umpired ejected him. All their options thwarted, the Yankees finally went on with the game and quickly went down in order in the bottom of the ninth, preserving their 5–4 loss and national shame.

C. W. McCall even recorded a song about it called "Pine Tar Wars," singing that all Martin does is cry and fight and kick dirt on the umpire.

So now we're gonna take
that Pine Tar Rag,
And rub it in ye'r face again.

Okay, it isn't exactly Cole Porter, but it has a certain appeal.

The Pine Tar Box Score

Kansas City	ab	r	h	rbi	New York	ab	r	h	rbi
Wilson cf	3	0	0	0	Campaneris 2b	4	1	2	0
Sheridan cf	2	0	0	0	Griffey 1b	0	0	0	0

Kansas City	ab	r	h	rbi	New York	ab	r	h	rbi
Simpson cf	0	0	0	0	Nettles 3b	3	0	0	0
Washington ss	5	1	1	0	Piniella rf	4	1	1	0
Brett 3b	5	1	3	2	Mumphrey cf	0	0	0	0
Pryor 3b	0	0	0	0	Wynegar c	0	0	0	0
McRae dh	4	0	0	0	Baylor dh	4	1	1	2
Otis rf	4	0	1	0	Winfield cf	4	1	3	2
Wathan 1b	3	2	1	0	Kemp lf	4	0	0	0
Roberts lf	3	0	2	0	Balboni 1b	2	0	0	0
Aikens 1b	1	0	0	0	Mattingly 1b	2	0	0	0

White 2b	4	1	2	2	Smalley ss	4	0	1	0
Slaught c	4	0	3	1	Cerone c	2	0	0	0
					Guidry cf	0	0	0	0
					Gamble ph	1	0	0	0
Totals	**38**	**5**	**13**	**5**		**34**	**4**	**8**	**4**

Kansas City 010 101 002-5
New York   010 003 000-4

GWRBI-Brett (10). DP-New York 1. LOB-Kansas City 8, New York 5.
2B-White, Slaught, Baylor. HR-Winfield (16), Brett (20).

Kansas City	**IP**	**H**	**R**	**ER**	**BB**	**K**
Black	6	7	4	4	0	2
Armstrong W, 6-6	2	1	0	0	2	0
Quisenberry S, 33	1	0	0	0	0	0
New York						
Rawley	5.1	10	3	3	2	2
Murray	3.1	2	1	1	0	2
Gossage L, 10-4	0	1	1	1	0	0
Frazier	.1	0	0	0	0	0

Gossage pitched to one batter in 9th.

T-2:52. A-33,944 (July 24); 1,245 (completion). U-(July 24):
HP-McClelland, 1B-Coble, 2B-Brinkman, 3B-Bremigan. U-(completion):
HP-Maloney, 1B-Welke, 2B-Phillips, 3B-Reed.

10. Mike Kekich and Fritz Peterson
swap wives (1972–73)

As mentioned earlier, one of Steinbrenner's first moves as owner was to order players with long hair to the barbershop. We can only imagine then what his reaction was when he found out that two of the players on the team he just bought had swapped wives.

What?!?! They swapped what? Wives? Don't they realize this could raise our insurance premiums? Wife-swapping? That's the most disgusting thing I've ever heard since I found out about the progressive income tax. It's an abomination. This decline of the nation's morality is just what our great President Nixon is fighting against. I wouldn't expect this from a Yankee in a million years. A Met, sure, but not a Yankee.

I told you those two needed haircuts.

Pitchers Mike Kekich and Fritz Peterson, as it turned out, had traded more than wives. In the most astounding trade in baseball history that did not involve agent Scott Boras, the two also traded children, pets, homes and cars. Although it's tempting to assign this scandal to Steinbrenner's watch, the trade actually took place late in the 1972 season (presumably after Mrs. Kekich cleared waivers), several months before George bought the team. The swap finally became public knowledge during spring training of 1973 when the two pitchers set the franchise standard for disgrace so low that Jeffrey Maier couldn't have crawled under it.

Said Yankees president Lee MacPhail when he learned of the trade: "We may have to call off Family Day this season."

Not surprisingly, the wife-swapping left-handers didn't last long with the Yankees. New York traded Kekich to Cleveland in mid-June of 1973 and dealt Peterson to Cleveland the following April. (Apparently, Cleveland was a rather tolerant organization in those days.) Kekich, who won ten games for New York in 1972, won only seven games the rest of his career. Peterson, who had averaged seventeen wins the four seasons prior to the family swap, won thirty-two more games before his career ended in 1976.

Peterson married Susanne Kekich and the couple had four children of their own. Mike Kekich's relationship with Marilyn Peterson, like his tenure with the Yankees, didn't last the 1973 season. He eventually went to medical school, telling *New York Times* columnist George Vecsey that when he told people he was in medical school, they replied, "I'm not letting you touch me."

Honorable Mention: *Ball Four* tarnishes the Yankees' image (spring 1970)

The most entertaining, revealing and honest book ever written about baseball, *Ball Four*, was Jim Bouton's diary of his 1969 season with the Seattle Pilots and the Houston Astros. But it also read like an early version of *The New York Yankees: Behind the Music.* Bouton pitched for the Yankees from 1962 to 1968, and thanks to his book we learned that Mickey Mantle had a drinking problem, Whitey Ford doctored the ball with whatever he could find, the Yankees were sexually promiscuous Peeping Toms and their owners were greedy skinflints.

A wonderful time capsule of baseball and America in the late '60s, *Ball Four* is "just" a baseball book the same way *The Grapes of Wrath* is just a book about picking peaches. The New York Public Library named it one of the most important books of the century. The Yankees, however, did not look at the book the same way. Shunning Bouton for years for "betraying" the team, New York failed to include him in old-timers' games for almost three decades.

The Astros no-hit the Yankees (June 11, 2003): It was a moment that transcended sports, like when the troops landed on D-day or when Neil Armstrong stepped on the moon or when Ruben beat Clay. On June 11, a record six Astros pitchers—Roy Oswalt and Billy Wagner plus household names Pete Munro, Kirk Saarloos, Brad Lidge and Octavio Dotel—combined to do what no pitcher or group of pitchers had done since Steinbrenner was in the 28 percent tax bracket. They no-hit the Yankees for nine innings.

The Combined No-Hitter Box Score

Houston	ab	r	h	rbi	New York	ab	r	h	rbi
Biggio cf	5	1	2	0	Soriano 2b	4	0	0	0
Blum 3b	5	1	1	0	Jeter ss	3	0	0	0
Bagwell 1b	5	1	2	0	Giambi dh	3	0	0	0

Kent 2b	4	0	1	0	Posada c	3	0	0	0
Berkman lf	4	2	1	2	Ventura 3b	3	0	0	0
Hidalgo rf	5	1	2	2	Trammell ph	1	0	0	0
Merced dh	5	1	1	0	Matsui cf	4	0	0	0
Vizcaino ss	2	0	1	1	Zeile 1b	2	0	0	0
Everett ss	1	0	0	0	Mondesi rf	3	0	0	0
Ausmus c	4	1	3	1	Rivera lf	3	0	0	0
Totals	**40**	**8**	**14**	**6**		**29**	**0**	**0**	**0**

Houston   112 000 112-8
New York   000 000 000-0

E-Jeter. LOB-Houston 8, New York 6. 2B-Biggio, Vizcaino, Hidalgo (2), Bagwell. 3B-Merced. HR-Berkman (12). SB-Soriano (18). SF-Vizcaino.

Houston	**IP**	**H**	**R**	**ER**	**BB**	**K**
Oswalt	1	0	0	0	0	2
Munro	2.2	0	0	0	2	3

Houston	**IP**	**H**	**R**	**ER**	**BB**	**K**
Saarloos	1.1	0	0	0	0	1
Lidge W, 4-0	2	0	0	0	0	2
Dotel	1	0	0	0	0	4

New York						
Weaver L, 3-5	6.1	10	5	5	1	2
Hammond	.2	0	0	0	0	1
Anderson	1	2	1	1	0	1
Reyes	1	2	2	2	1	0

WP- Weaver, Anderson, Dotel. HBP-Giambi (by Munro). T-2:52. A-29,905.

Reggie returns (May 10, 1982): Even though the Yankees went to the World Series three times in five years with the Straw That Stirs the Drink in the lineup, Steinbrenner let Reggie leave as a free agent after the 1981 season. He returned with the Angels in May when he was hitting just .173 with no home runs. In the seventh inning he homered off the façade in right field and winked at catcher Rick Cerone as he crossed the plate, while the stadium echoed with the sweetest words ever chanted in Yankee Stadium, "Steinbrenner Sucks! Steinbrenner Sucks! Steinbrenner Sucks!"

The Dodgers sweep the Yankees (October 1963): The Yankees gave one of the most feeble World Series performances that didn't involve a Fox prime-time star singing the national anthem. The first five Yankees struck out to open the series and things never got better for them. New York not only was swept by the Dodgers, it never held a lead in the series and trailed in all but six of the thirty-six innings. The Yankees scored only four runs and hit just .171, with Mickey Mantle turning in one of his worst series, batting .133.

Bob Welch fans Reggie (October 11, 1978): Welch had less than four months in the majors when the Dodgers brought him in to protect a 4–3 lead in Game 2 of the 1978 World Series with the go-ahead run on base. Reggie worked the count full and fouled off three 3-2 pitches before Welch finally struck him out on pure heat to end the game. The strikeout brought the Dodger Stadium crowd to its feet—or at least the ones who hadn't left in the seventh inning to beat the traffic.

Maz homers (October 13, 1960): The Yankees outscored the Pirates 55–27 in the 1960 World Series and so dominated them that when Bobby Richardson was named the series MVP he became the only MVP for the losing team in series history. None of that mattered, though, when Bill Mazeroski homered in the bottom of the ninth of Game 7 to give Pittsburgh a 10–9 victory and the world championship. Despite the stunning reversal of fortune, the Yankees responded with nothing but class. They fired manager Casey Stengel the next week.

There also was the time the Babe was caught trying to steal second base to end the 1926 World Series and the year Burdette beat the Yankees three times to win the World Series and the time Jack Chesbro threw a game-ending wild pitch to decide the 1904 pennant and . . . Pardon me. Before continuing with this book, I'm just going to rest a moment here with a big grin on my face.

CHAPTER 6

Yankees Fans Are from Mars . . .

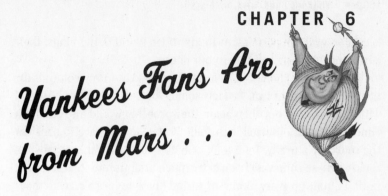

No one enjoys filing an income tax return, but at least the IRS isn't constantly phoning you at home to brag about how much money they took during the 1998 tax year. Yankees fans, however, are under the impression that no newspapers ever print the American League standings. You have as good a chance of hearing a humble Yankees fan as you do hearing a woman's voice calling into a sports talk radio show.

They are as persistent as a telemarketer working on straight commission. No matter the setting, no matter the occasion, if you sit next to Yankees fans, they'll brag about the team until your ears start bleeding.

Yeah, yeah, I know. The Yankees won 125 games in 1998, including a four-game sweep of the Padres in the World Series, which they've won a total of twenty-six times. And yeah, I know, Babe Ruth still holds the American League record for most career home runs and Mickey Mantle holds the record for most home runs by a switch-hitter. And yeah, I know, there are seventeen players wearing a Yankees cap in the Hall of Fame. Now, will you shut up, Father, and listen to my confession?

Heaven forbid you bring up the 2004 postseason or say something derogatory about the Yankees. If you don't genuflect before the Yankees altar and ask permission to kiss their World Series rings, their fans want John Ashcroft to tap your phone.

Believe me, I know. I poke fun at the Yankees in my columns for ESPN.com. A lot of fun. In fact, some would say that I'm obsessed with the Yankees, but then again they probably would also say John Hinckley Jr. was obsessed with Jodie Foster, so you have to consider the source. Naturally, I get a lot of hate mail from Yankees fans because of these columns. I don't pay much attention to it, at least not until it builds up every month or so and I have to hire a crew to move the piles blocking my car in the garage.

What I find most interesting in the hate mail is that the vast majority of Yankees fans simply cannot fathom the possibility that anyone could hate their team unless he or she also roots for the Red Sox. It's simply beyond their capacity to imagine that there are people all over the world who hate the Yankees for their own very legitimate reasons, and not just because they live in Boston.

Whenever I write something anti-Yankee, their fans always assume that I live across the street from Fenway Park, speak with a thick Boston accent and am such a regular at the Cask 'n Flagon that when I walk in, I'm greeted by everyone like Norm was on *Cheers*. This is a typical letter:

> *Die, Red Sox @#$@&&, die!*
>
> *Suck this, you Boston @#&%! You're so @##*&% jealous of the Yankees' twenty-six championships you make me want to PUKE! What kind of hole did you crawl out from? If you write any more @#%$& crap about the greatest team and the greatest fans in the world, I'll personally drive over to your house and rip off your @#$@&* testicles and stuff them down your throat until you choke to death on them. YOU AND MANNY AND PEDRO AND EVERYONE WHO PLAYS ON THE RED SOX OR EVER PLAYED FOR THEM OR WILL EVER PLAY FOR THEM SUCK!!!!*
>
> *P.S. Your mother reminded me to ask whether you're coming to dinner with the rest of the family this weekend. She's cooking up a big turkey, so don't be late. Love, Dad.*

They're wrong, of course. People hate the Yankees everywhere. And I mean everywhere. Brazilian researchers recently discovered an Indian tribe in so remote a part of the Amazon that these natives had never been exposed to Western society. Although I cannot absolutely, positively vouch for this, I believe the only words they were able to understand were "Jeter sucks."

Yankee Stadium: Where Loyalty Is a Slogan

Yankees fans not only think their team is the greatest in the history of sports, they consider themselves to be the most knowledgeable, the most loyal and the most supportive fans in the history of the game. This is understandable given that the World's Greatest Fans have absolutely no appreciation for any baseball played outside the Bronx. If it didn't take place within range of John Sterling's voice, it's as if it never happened. They refuse to acknowledge that fans in other cities love baseball and the local team as much as they do.

Are Yankees fans the most supportive in baseball? Sure, they've drawn staggering crowds the past couple seasons, but let's look back a little further. From 1987 to 1994, the Minnesota Twins outdrew the Yankees, this despite the fact that New York City's population is roughly five times that of the Twin Cities. Granted, that was during a span when the Twins won two world championships and New York failed to even reach the postseason (sigh, weren't those the salad days?), but fan support for the Yankees has been lacking even when the team won championships. The Yankees went to the World Series three times from 1962 to 1965 and yet were outdrawn during that span by the expansion Mets, who averaged 113 losses and finished in last place each season, a combined 195½ games out of first place.

If you want the most supportive fans in baseball, go to St. Louis, where the Cardinals have outdrawn the Yankees over the past quarter century even though St. Louis's population barely matches the number of New York City's homeless.

Loyal fans? England and France showed more support for Czechoslovakia in 1939 than the World's Greatest Fans show when their team loses.

On September 22, 1966, the Yankees drew 413 fans for a game. No, that's not a misprint—413 fans. I think Jeter has slept with more people than that. Four hundred and thirteen fans! And that was just two years after the Yankees had gone to the World Series. The crowd was so small that Hall of Fame broadcaster Red Barber instructed the TV cameras to pan the nearly empty stadium. (The Yankees responded in typical fashion by firing him.) When the Yankees had losing seasons from 1990 to 1992, they were outdrawn by every team in the league except Cleveland, Seattle, Milwaukee and Detroit.

Even during their supposed heyday, that great "golden era" of New York baseball in the '50s when the Yankees reached the World Series so often that it should have been printed on their pocket schedules, they were a disappointment at the gate. From 1952 to 1962, when the Yankees went to the World Series nine times and won it six times, New York was outdrawn by the Milwaukee Braves. That's right, the Yankees were outdrawn by Bud Selig's hometown, *which didn't even have a team in 1952*.

Don't blame it on competition from the Giants and the Dodgers, either. The Yankees won the pennant in 1958 when the Giants and Dodgers moved to California and left them as the only team in New York—and their attendance still went down.

And here's a stat you'll never see on *Yankeeography*: When Roger Maris took the field for the final game of the 1961 season with a chance to break Ruth's coveted home run record, only 23,154 fans bothered going to Yankee Stadium. In other words, there were more empty seats in Yankee Stadium that day than there were in Fenway Park—and the Red Sox were playing in New York.

(It wasn't just the Yankees that were a disappointing draw, though. The next time Doris Kearns Goodwin, Roger Kahn or Ken Burns start talking about the glorious golden age of New York baseball, remind them that there were 20,000 empty seats in the Polo Grounds for Bobby Thomson's Shot Heard 'Round the World, the most famous game in history. Jackie Robinson's major league debut, the most important game in baseball history, drew just 25,623 fans—and that was for a season opener. No wonder the Giants and Dodgers fled New York for the West Coast.)

Despite playing in the nation's largest metropolitan area and despite playing in one of the game's biggest stadiums, it took until 1999 before the Yankees actually cracked the 3 million mark. Not until after the Yankees had played ninety-six seasons, won twenty-four world championships and won 114 games in a season did their fans respond with an attendance level that had already been reached forty-six times by thirteen other teams, including the Florida Marlins. When they led the majors in attendance in 2003, it was the first time they had done so in more than half a century.

If we break down attendance by percentage of population, the picture for our good, loyal New York fans looks as bleak as the streets surrounding Yankee Stadium.

New York is the largest city in the country, with an overall market of 21 million people. Obviously, because New York has two teams, we should split that in two, giving the Yankees and the Mets each a surrounding market size of 10.5 million, still easily the highest in the country. So even though the Yankees led the majors in attendance with approximately 3.8 million fans in 2004, that's just barely one fan per every three citizens. Only three teams had lower ratios (the Mets, Tigers and Orioles) and they were all losers. By contrast, the Reds drew more fans than there are residents of the Cincinnati metro area.

But the Yankees fans are the best and most loyal in the game, right?

The Decline of Western Civilization

In 2001, a game between the Yankees and the Twins at the Metrodome was delayed twelve minutes when Minnesota fans pelted left fielder Chuck Knoblauch with hot dogs. Twins manager Tom Kelly apologized for the fans' actions and then-Minnesota governor Jesse Ventura went so far as to send a letter to Steinbrenner apologizing.

Predictably, the World's Greatest Fans also were appalled by such behavior.

Such things would never be tolerated in Yankee Stadium, the House That Love Built. The only things we ever throw are rose petals and women's panties to our favorite players and spare change and nonperishable foods into the collection baskets held by the smiling security guards.

Right. Former Orioles pitcher Mike Flanagan once said, "I could never play in New York. The first time I ever came into a game there, I got in the bullpen cart and they told me to lock the doors."

Other ballparks have strict rules about playing pepper. Yankee Stadium has strict rules about employing pepper spray.

During the 1995 division series between the Mariners and Yankees, New York's first trip to the postseason in fourteen years, I was sitting in the auxiliary press box, which was placed among the fans down the third base line. It wasn't a bad seat at all. Nice view of the game. Good feel for the excitement of the crowd. The only problem was when some fans began chanting about stealing our TV monitors.

And that was in the relatively tame reserved section where the stockbrokers and surgeons sit. The fans were much worse in the bleachers.

"We made a pitching change, I think, in the sixth inning [of Game 2] and I remember the grounds crew came out with fifty-five-gallon plastic garbage drums and they were literally filling them up because there was so much crap they were throwing on the outfield," former Mariners right fielder Jay Buhner remembers. "It was out of control. They were throwing two-liter bottles of pop from the upper deck and they were hitting the ground and exploding. The fans were throwing everything. Batteries, golf balls, marbles, coins—friggin' everything. It was almost like *Rollerball*.

"You're standing out there thinking, 'This is crazy. What's to keep these people from jumping out on the field?' It wasn't a very comfortable environment. The crowd was getting out of control. I still felt safe because they've got so many cops there and they do such a great job so you don't really worry about it, but it's still in the back of your mind. I remember after the crew picked up all the garbage, the umpires came out and said, 'Do us a favor, don't say anything to the crowd. Don't entice them. Don't pay any attention to them. Don't flip them off. Junior, you especially, don't spin your glove on your finger, don't play along with them. Just ignore them until they die out. Please.'"

That game may have marked the heaviest deluge, but Buhner says the World's Greatest Fans used to throw so many coins at him each game during the regular season that he and Ken Griffey Jr. would each pick $6 to $7 in quarters off the grass. Naturally, the fans heckled them for being greedy.

Yes, Yankee Stadium's bleacher bums *are* devoted and knowledgeable baseball fans. Their roll-call ritual in the first inning (chanting the name of each player until he acknowledges them with a wave of the glove) is one of baseball's best traditions, next to Cubs fans passing out under the El tracks. They can be clever enough that even the opposing players who are recipients of this abuse have to smile in appreciation. But the fans also can be so crude that Suge Knight would flee for the safety of the family section.

"They can totally take a player out of his element and out of his game," Buhner says. "And for a young kid who isn't used to that, they can intimidate him."

"One time during batting practice, some kid who was nine or eleven years old was yelling at Pedro Muñoz to throw him a ball," relief pitcher Eddie Guardado says. "He wasn't asking him, he was telling him. 'Pedro, throw me a ball.' I was new to the majors so I said, 'Why don't you throw him a ball?' And he said, 'No. They're jerks so I never throw them the ball.'

"Finally, he gets tired of hearing the kid and throws him a baseball. And the kid catches the ball and yells back, 'F— you!' and then gives him the finger."

It's their way of saying thank you.

Berlitz Yankee

Unlike the Inuit, who supposedly have fifty words to describe snow, Yankees fans have a more limited language. They rely on one word, "sucks," to convey a wide range of ideas, emotions and preferences through inflection, expression and the surrounding words in the sentence. At first the language can seem confusing, but by practicing a few helpful phrases you soon will be able to communicate like a native.

Yankees	English
"You suck!"	"Excuse me."
"Suck me!"	"Please."
"Your mother sucks!"	"Thank you."
"Your father sucks!"	"You're welcome."
"This sucks!"	"How many days have those hot dogs been sitting on the grill?"
"Ted Williams sucks!"	"Does your hotel have air conditioning?"
"Manny sucks!"	"Where may I exchange my second baseman who strikes out too much for the best player in the league?"
"Curt Schilling sucks!"	"Could I see your menu? Wait, on second thought, I'll just order two of everything you serve."
"Piazza sucks!"	"Heads up! Duck!"

Yankees	English
"Al Leiter sucks!"	"Is this the express train to Queens or can I get off before it reaches the middle of nowhere?"
"Jose Reyes sucks!"	"Is there a pharmacy nearby where I can buy a dandruff shampoo? I can't seem to get this ticker tape out of my hair."
"Shea Stadium sucks!"	"Where may I throw away my garbage?"
"The Mets suck!"	"No, thank you, I'm looking for fashionable clothes that fit and are much more expensive. Do you have anything in pinstripes?"
"Steinbrenner sucks!"	"Steinbrenner sucks!"

The World's Greatest Fans aren't as brutal as they used to be, but it's not because Yankees fans have become more genteel. It's just that the Yankees, in a rare display of wisdom, have banned beer sales in the bleachers, beefed up security and set up so many surveillance cameras that even the Department of Homeland Security probably thinks it's a little intrusive. Even so, they threw so much garbage on the field during Game 6 of the 2004 ALCS that major league security stationed riot police at the edge of the field, giving new meaning to the term "guarding the lines."

And it's not like the beer restrictions completely muffle the fans.

"They'll dig up stuff you can't believe," Cleveland outfielder Matt Lawton says with admiration. "They do their homework. They'll bring up your parents' names, your sister's name, your cousin's name. They'll bring up people you never even knew you were related to. One day they brought up my grandfather's name. I was like, how do they know what my grandfather's name is?"

Before each game, Bob Sheppard warns that any fan who interferes with the play of the game will be ejected from the stadium, a warning as strictly enforced as the city's jaywalking ordinances. During New York's 1996 playoff series with Baltimore, twelve-year-old Jeffrey Maier reached out and grabbed Jeter's fly ball away from right fielder Tony Tarasco, pulling the ball into the stands and giving the Yankees a disputed home run. Everyone in the country clearly saw on the replays that Maier had interfered with the ball and that Jeter's home run was totally undeserved. Instead of being ejected, he was literally given the key to New York, championed throughout the city, invited to appear on *Regis, Rosie* and *Letterman* and chauffeured to the next game in a limousine. He even hired a publicist.

And what is generally forgotten is that Maier, showing the sort of defense not seen in Yankee Stadium since Reggie played right field, dropped the ball. Another fan picked up the ball, and in tried-and-true fashion, refused to give it back to Maier. Instead, he sold it for a couple thousand dollars.

Which is yet another example of just how exasperating the Yankees are. When a Cubs fan interferes with a fly ball, it results in the team collapsing, blowing a seemingly insurmountable lead, losing a postseason series, missing the World Series for the fifty-eighth time in a row and plunging the city into such drunken despair not even Dr. Phil can reach them. When a Yankees fan does it, it results in a home run that propels them into the World Series and puts a couple thousand bucks into some undeserving fan's checking account.

Behind the Yankees: Jeffrey Maier Comes Clean

"Hell no, I wasn't twelve when I caught that 'home run' in the 1996 playoffs. I was thirty-six years old and part of Steinbrenner's secret midget plan. I never liked Steinbrenner but I've got to give credit where it's due—the Boss never missed a trick. When fans in the bleacher sections started getting a little rough and their behavior began discouraging attendance, he hired midgets on the sly to dress as kids and sit out there to make it look more family-oriented. Cashman and Kim Ng scoured the country for dwarves, signing them away from circuses, department store Christmas displays and community theater productions of *The Wizard of Oz*. Me and Vern Troyer were two of the first guys they hired. And you know the way Steinbrenner is, never sign five guys when you can sign fifty. They wound up stocking so many of us that Ringling Bros. had to shut down for a month.

"Anyway, grabbing that home run ball was just quick thinking on my part and I had no idea it would put me in the national spotlight. But I'm a pro—I honed my improvisation skills at the Second City in Chicago—so I knew how to run with the story. I told everyone I was twelve and a lifelong Yankees fan (actually, I'm an octopus-carrying Detroit Redwings fans) and they bought it hook, line and sinker. I was the toast of the town for a week. I was on Regis and the *Today* show, *Saturday Night Live* asked me to host and Giuliani offered me a position on his campaign staff.

"That's when the trouble began. See, Steinbrenner had me typecast—he wanted me to continue playing this teenage dork, but I had higher aspirations. I had visions of being a designated hitter—you know, like Eddie Gaedel—and pinch-hitting anytime the Yanks needed a walk. Or at the very least, I said, make me a batboy, let me hand Derek a special hand-carved bat like in *The Natural* or high-five Bernie after a home run. Anything to get my picture in the paper occasionally. But the Boss wouldn't go for any of it. The best he offered me was a job as the team mascot so

Torre could rub my head for luck between innings. Torre refused, saying it was insulting to the team, demeaning to dwarves, beneath him as a manager and besides, he already had Zimmer.

"So, I left the team and returned to my life in the theater. The work isn't as steady—Peter Dinklage gets all the good dwarves parts—but it's what I love. I'm touring with Chuck Knoblauch in *The Odd Couple* and I have no regrets. Miss working for the Yankees? Christ, no! Do you know what it's like to shave four times a day?"

The Bronx Jeer

Win and Yankees fans shower you with love. Lose and they shower you with other four-letter words. The World's Greatest Fans heckled Ed Whitson so mercilessly during the 1986 season that he began hyperventilating before one start and became such a mental wreck that then-manager Lou Piniella eventually had him pitch exclusively on the road. He also started wearing disguises on his drive home.

Imagine what it would have been like had he had a losing record instead of his 15-10 mark with the Yankees.

The World's Greatest Fans heckled Clemens relentlessly when he pitched for the Red Sox (*"You suck, Roger!"*) then embraced him after he forced his trade to New York in 1999 (*"You rock, Roger!"*). They lovingly cheered him and gave him a standing ovation each time he left the mound for what could have been his final game at the end of the 2003 season (*"We are not worthy!"*). But as soon as he changed his mind and came out of retirement to sign with Houston, the New York headlines referred to him as "Ass-tro," undoubtedly to the delight of the fans.

They booed Maris the season he hit sixty-one home runs. *Next time do it in 154 games, you bum!* Some booed Winfield in 1984 when he hit .340 and went into the final week of the season leading the league in batting. And when Winfield appeared in the Macy's Thanksgiving Day Parade the month after his 1-for-22 performance in the 1981 World Series, he seriously considered wearing a bullet-proof vest, writing in his 1988 autobiography, "I'd be an easy target traveling the parade route down Fifth Avenue."

They booed the team during the 2004 ALCS. Granted, the Yankees embarrassed themselves by choking away a 3–0 lead, but would the World's Greatest Fans really boo their own for falling one win short of the World Series?

Even Jeter, normally worshipped with the sort of reverence reserved for a religious leader or a lead guitarist, felt the fickle nature of the World's Greatest Fans. More than any other single player, Jeter was primarily responsible for lifting the Yankees back to dominance, leading them to the postseason every year of his career. But when he dared to fall into an 0-for-32 slump in April of 2004, the World's Greatest Fans let him have it, booing him without regard to his previous contributions. Imagine, booing Jeter. How did they follow that up? Spray-painting graffiti on the Statue of Liberty, urinating against the Empire State Building and dumping their beer cans in Central Park?

Not that they'll allow anyone else to slight Jeter. Oh, no. Blue Jays catcher Ken Huckaby had the misfortune of accidentally injuring Jeter on the opening day of the 2003 season in a freak play. Hustling to cover third base because the Toronto infielders were playing an extreme shift on Jason Giambi, Huckaby fell on Jeter while tagging him when the Yankee captain slid into the bag. The collision separated Jeter's shoulder and knocked him out for six weeks. Although it was a complete accident, Huckaby nonetheless attempted to apologize to Jeter on the phone and in person for what happened, only to be rudely rebuffed. "Jeter didn't say anything. He just stood there and stared back at me." Worse, however, was the reaction of Yankees fans, who filled Huckaby's mailbox with hate mail and death threats.

"They wrote things like, 'You better not stick your head out of the hotel when you're in New York,'" Huckaby says. "They took it very seriously. They are very fanatical about their players and in their eyes, they thought I probably cost them a chance to win a World Series."

Hey Huckaby, you @&$%#!

After what you did to Jeter's shoulder, you better watch out. If you ever step foot into any of the five boroughs that make up the greatest city in the world, I will personally arrange to have you "trip" off the observation deck of the Empire State Building, "slip" off the Staten Island Ferry, "fall" under a subway train or experience several other unpleasant and deadly encounters with some of the many popular tourist attractions that make New York the Big Apple. And if you think that's cruel and unusual punishment, just be glad the city no longer has a crime problem. If David Dinkins still was mayor, you could look forward to a run-in with a gang wilding in Central Park. You suck!!!!

Sincerely,
Rudy Giuliani

Giuliani, of course, is the Yankees official mascot and the most notorious of their celebrity fans. He attended so many games at Yankee Stadium, it was hard to tell whether he was New York's mayor or Torre's bench coach. If he wasn't bending arms to try to get the city to build a new stadium for his good buddy George, he was drafting every Yankee available for his rotisserie baseball team.

Another celebrity fan is Billy Crystal, who boasts about his lifelong love affair with the Yankees, though curiously he wore a Mets cap throughout the 1991 movie *City Slickers*. Hmmm. That choice couldn't have had anything to do with the Mets being a contender and the Yankees being in last place when the movie was filmed, could it?

And then there's *Sex and the City* star Sarah Jessica Parker. After the Marlins whipped the Yankees in the 2003 World Series, she stood outside the New York clubhouse weeping like Bill Mazeroski at a screening of *Field of Dreams*.

Perhaps Parker was crying because she was starring in a TV show about four gorgeous women having regular sex in New York City and yet somehow in six years none of them slept with Jeter. Otherwise I can't understand what could possibly justify a Yankees fan ever crying. You can understand tears running down the logo-painted cheeks of Red Sox, Cubs, White Sox, Cleveland, Mariners, Giants, Padres, Expos, Astros or Rangers fans. I mean, those fans have *suffered*.

But a Yankees fan crying? After four world championships in the past eight years and twenty-six overall, how could any single loss provoke tears of sadness? A Yankee fan crying over losing one World Series is as unseemly as Donald Trump crying over Rockefeller Center blocking the view of St. Patrick's Cathedral.

Get over it, baby.

A Day in the Bleachers, a Night in Hell

In researching his recent bestseller, *Rats,* Robert Sullivan pored over books, journals and articles during the day and then went to lower Manhattan each night for an entire summer to sit in a stinking, garbage-strewn alleyway while wearing night goggles to observe the rodents root through the garbage and waste. He even tracked the rats by following their droppings and inspecting their holes.

Hah! He had it easy. To research this book, I sat in the Yankee Stadium bleachers for an entire game. By the seventh inning, I felt so dirty that I needed more than a shower; I needed sandblasting. It was like sitting next to Dick Cheney on the Senate floor.

And no, I'm not making up any of the following. It is all too sadly true. . . .

"If this is your first game," the nearby fan clanging the cowbell in section 39 said, "welcome to hell."

He was joking, of course. This was not hell—the Devil doesn't require that many security guards. There were enough off-duty cops manning the right-field bleachers each game to fill every Dunkin' Donuts in the tristate area. The guards eyed the crowd constantly while a woman cop patrolled up and down the aisles and generally dared anyone to make her day—a female Clint Eastwood. Granted, that's a pretty grim image, but not as grim a sight as seeing many of the fans challenging the limits of their XXXXL Bleacher Creatures T-shirts.

Anniversary Presents, Traditional and Yankees

True Yankees fans can tell you instinctively how many home runs Mickey Mantle hit in his career (536), DiMaggio's career batting average (.325) and exactly where they were when Reggie hit three home runs in Game 6 of the 1977 World Series. Like other fans, though, they have a little trouble with more trivial facts, such as their wedding anniversaries.

Even if they do remember, what do you get the fan who has everything? And who has time to think of a present, let alone buy one, when the pennant race is heating up and the Red Sox come to town? Fortunately, there is help. Here are the traditional presents for anniversaries, plus a special category of appropriate gifts just for Yankees fans.

Anniversary	Traditional	Yankees
First	Paper	"We're No. 1" giant foam puffy hand
Second	Cotton	Adjustable cap
Third	Leather	Yankees Visa card beach towel
Fourth	Flowers	"I ♥ the Yankees" license plates
Fifth	Wood	Scoreboard announcement
Sixth	Candy	Stirrup socks
Seventh	Copper	Yogi bobblehead
Eighth	Bronze	Old-timers jersey
Ninth	Pottery	Satin jacket
Tenth	Tin	Marriage counseling

While the abundant security prevented any physical violence (after all, the Red Sox weren't in town), the verbal abuse was overwhelming. The Mariners were playing, so before the game a group of bleacher regulars thoughtfully distributed sheets of insults translated into Japanese so fans could heckle Ichiro in his own language. Among others, there were translations for "gay boy," "f— you, bitch," "penis," "rectum" and the always appropriate "C'mon up here and get your ass kicked." A couple Japanese fans huddled with them, pointing out a large number of errors and providing the correct translations until one fan turned to another and said, "We won't get it right anyway, so it doesn't really matter."

So, every time Ichiro ran out to right field, he was serenaded with a chorus of mispronounced, incorrect Japanese insults, which no doubt must have left him very confused.

"Why do they keep chanting that I'm a 'Very happy young man'? This is true, but why do they care? And why do they keep saying that I 'inhale'?"

Obviously, Ichiro wasn't the only one singled out. As their oft-repeated chant went whenever the fan stopped clanging his cowbell: "Yankee baseball, Mets suck, Seattle sucks, Ichiro sucks, right field sucks, everyone sucks!" *Everyone sucks* is the mantra of the bleachers. And by everyone, they meant *everyone,* including the fans. Whenever a man walked by with a woman wearing anything more revealing than a burqa, they yelled, "Your girlfriend is a slut!" and "Show your tits!"

The sixth inning brought a particularly nice Bleacher Creature tradition. When the team plays "Y.M.C.A." at the end of the inning, they always sing along with their own wacky, homophobic lyrics. I couldn't make them all out while listening in the stands, but according to Dean Chadwin in his book *Those Damn Yankees,* the revised lyrics go like this:

Gay man
Get up off of your knees
I said, gay man
What a mass of disease
I said, gay man

Don't touch me please
Because you have got a disease

Why are you gay?
(You suck! You suck! You suck!)"

And so on in similar uproarious fashion.

What makes all this routine especially clever is that the creatures pick out an unsuspecting fan each night to whom they direct the lyrics, turning each victim into a quivering mass of Jell-O. Yes, it sounds harsh, but at least on the night I was there the victim fully deserved it. After all, he was wearing a shirt with orange stripes.

So as the stadium sound people cued up the "Y.M.C.A." recording, several of the Bleacher Creatures sidled up to the designated "Gay Man" with big smiles, welcoming him into the fold. As he smiled back, a fan thoroughly enjoying it all whispered to his friend, "He has no idea what's going to happen."

No, he didn't. As they sang their lyrics, he sat there absolutely stunned, looking as if he had been caught in the headlights by a speeding van of IRS auditors. He appeared ready to cry as the lyrics went on and on and on until it seemed like it could get no worse.

And then someone threw a drink in his face.

Now, I don't want to give the impression that the Bleacher Creatures are disrespectful. Not at all. When the Yankees played a recording of Kate Smith singing "God Bless America" during the seventh-inning stretch, two fans held up a U.S. flag and another fan stood at attention and saluted it while wearing a T-shirt that read "We Banged Your Mom." And as soon as the recording finished, the creatures chanted, "Kate Smith sucks! Kate Smith sucks!"

I tell you, it made me proud to be an American.

Oh, and they also chanted welcoming phrases like "Our Jap is better than your Jap!" when Ichiro came to bat, "Where's your green card!" whenever a Hispanic fan dared look at them from the reserved section and "Jump, jump!" whenever anyone appeared near the top of the upper deck.

As rough as any of this sounds, the fans' behavior is actually better than it used to be. The Yankees cut off beer sales in the bleachers several years ago to reduce the fights, though the bleachers are no more free of alcohol than Chicago was during Prohibition. Fans come staggering into the section like Keith Richards at 4 a.m. and also smuggle in booze. When I was there a couple fans handed a man some cash to go retrieve some booze, and minutes later he was back with a fifth of Bacardi hidden in his jacket. The only surprise was he didn't toss the bottle at Ichiro's head when it was empty.

The really sad part is the bleachers are pretty much the only section parents can affordably take their kids to (tickets are $10, compared to $40 at the nearest reserved section over), but the language is so coarse that if they did so, Child Protective Services would probably have them arrested. There were very few kids in the bleachers the night I was there, though one couple had brought a boy who looked to be about twelve years old. The boy's head was shaved and his beer T-shirt barely covered his ample belly, making him look like a younger version of David Wells. One man loudly saluted Mini-Boomer as the fan of the game, christening him "the Bouncer" and yelling that "the Bouncer drinks more beer in a day than most people drink in a week."

Both the boy and his guardians beamed at this compliment, as if the kid had just been named to the school's honor roll.

And the thing is, the Yankees and the New York media are incredibly proud of these guys. While championing those fans' undeniable passion and loyalty, they bring up only the roll call and the clever chants while conveniently ignoring the incredibly offensive behavior. (Even those chants don't seem quite so clever when you realize that they've been working on them for years.)

Look, we're all adults and heckling the players is a well-established tradition at every ballpark from Little League ("We want a pitcher not a belly-itcher") to the American League. And I'm not advocating that teams should ban the word "sucks" on T-shirts or in chants—the word is now so broadly acceptable that you hear it in kindergarten as often as "I have to go pee." (Besides, I don't necessarily disagree with their assessment of the Kate Smith recording.) The last thing we want is to limit heckling to such politically correct phrases as "Two, four, six, eight, who do we appreciate? The Red Sox!" And I know the fans at Fenway can be just as bad.

But good lord. Are we really supposed to admire a group of fans who sing a nightly "Gang Bang" tune, the lyrics of which center on naming various players and how thoroughly they participated in gang bangs at young ages?

The one saving grace is that for all their arrogance—the self-satisfied smirk is as much a Yankees tradition as the interlocking NY logo—New York fans can never truly enjoy their victories.

Sure, there is an undeniable pleasure in rooting for a winning team and in being able to look down on opposing fans with equal measures of superiority and disdain. But that's also the Ruthian draw-back in rooting for the Yankees (along with high ticket prices, over-priced concessions and crude neighbors). The true pleasure in sports comes not from simply winning but from watching a team overcome adversity to win in the end. The joy of sports is never the final desti-nation, it's the journey. It's experiencing the highs and lows, and ap-preciating those highs all the more because of the awful lows.

The World's Greatest Fans can't know that. The Yankees have been so successful, they are so rich and so stocked with talent, that any-thing less than a World Series victory is a complete disappointment. And by the same token, if they win, there is no real sense of accom-plishment. As George Costanza stresses on the old *Seinfeld* episode when Jeter and Bernie point out to him that they won the World Series: "Yes, but it took you six games."

It's too easy being a Yankees fan. Anyone can root for a team that wins all the time. The test of a real fan is whether you have the char-acter to stick with your team through thick and thin. Anyone can be loyal to a team when it wins a World Series, but the question is whether you still love them when your parents hang up on the one phone call you're allowed from jail after being arrested for slashing the tires of the opposing shortstop's car again.

Which brings us to the subject of our next chapter . . . Boston Red Sox fans and their rivalry with the Yankees.

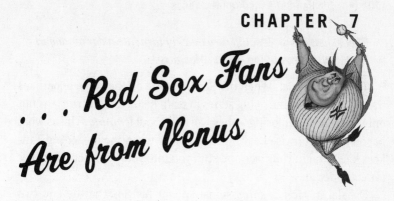

CHAPTER 7

... Red Sox Fans Are from Venus

On the eve of the 2004 American League championship series between the Yankees and the Red Sox, lifelong Boston fan Dave Dybala sent me this e-mail:

> I have a question for you. What would cause more pain: If the Sox either lose in heartbreaking fashion again in Game 7 against the Yanks or in the World Series, or if they actually win the World Series?
>
> I figure that if they do win, the death rate would spike because there are probably millions of sick and/or elderly New Englanders who are hanging alive ONLY to witness the Sox win it all, something so rare that nothing could be better. If the Sox do win it, the elderly or sick would think, "What else is worth living for at this point?" They could just close their eyes, not fight their respective diseases, and just rest happily in peace. Also, there would be the heartache and pain of family members realizing that the best day of their husbands'/fathers'/grandfathers' lives, is not their wedding day, not the birth of their children, but the day the Sox won it all.
>
> I honestly think that could be the mentality in New England when that point arrives. Not to mention the deaths due to riots.

Chaos, just chaos. It could very quickly turn into a darker day in Boston than that of the Boston Massacre.

Think about that. When the Red Sox were on the verge of perhaps the greatest, most satisfying series in team history, their true fans not only worried about losing—they worried about *winning*. This is what happens to otherwise healthy, sane people when the @#$&-ing Yankees kick sand in your face and stuff you into your high school locker for eight decades.

Dybala, in fact, is so passionate about his Sox that he and two friends showed up at the ballpark at ten at night to camp outside for tickets to the next day's game against the Yankees. That doesn't sound too odd until you understand that they didn't do this for one of the playoff games against the Yankees in October, they did it for a spring training game in March.

Evidently, competition in their Rotisserie Baseball League is *very* intense.

"This is the first meeting between the Red Sox and the Yankees since everything went down last fall," Larry Scott told me before that 2004 spring game. "I think it will have the intensity of a playoff game. It's not your average spring training game."

Well, he was wrong about that. Despite the high hopes, high prices (at least two tickets sold for $400) and hyperbole, it *was* your average spring training game. Johnny Damon (perhaps attending the cast wrap party for *The Passion of the Christ*) didn't play a single inning. Heck, it was such a meaningless game Ben Affleck didn't even show up.

Dybala and his friends didn't care. They were present at the beginning for the season when the Red Sox finally reversed the curse, evened the score with the @#$&-ing Yankees and changed the entire dynamics of their rivalry.

Codependency Is a Many Splendored Thing

Red Sox fans have always hated the Yankees. It's not enough to wear a Red Sox jersey or cap, devout fans must wear the ubiquitous "Yankees Suck!" and "Jeter Swallows" T-shirts. There is even a collection of unofficial Yankees Hater baseball caps, in colors and styles specifically designed for fans in different cities (I think they have a couple just for Hillary Rodham Clinton, depending on which stadium she's trying to appeal to voters in).

"We've sold caps in every single state in the U.S.," says Michael Moorby, who produces and sells the caps on his Web site, Yankeeshater .com. "The people are out there. People really like to see the Yankees fail. It's becoming a booming market. . . . We have a lot of parents buying stuff for their kids. We have a bunch of baby portraits with the kids in the cap. I'm not kidding—it runs deep. People tell stories, 'My father was a Yankee hater and his father was a Yankee hater.' "

Red Sox fans have joined themselves to Yankees fans like a kidney patient hooking himself to a dialysis machine, only with more pain and mental anguish usually involved over the years. No matter the occasion, Boston fans instinctively turn their thoughts to the Yankees.

"Yankees suck! Yankees suck! Yankees suck!"

"That's a very beautiful thought, Patrick, and I'm sure your dear Mary is thinking the exact same thing wherever she is. But the priest says you need to step away from the casket now."

Although they battled each other for the American League pennant on the final weekend of the 1904 season, the Yankees–Red Sox rivalry stems from Boston's sale of Babe Ruth to New York. The Red Sox immediately began paying for that original sin—they finished behind New York the next twenty-six seasons by an average of twenty-seven games a year. Playing their normal nineteen games per season against the Yankees, the Red Sox could win every meeting for the next fifty-five years and still finish behind New York in the combined standings since the Ruth trade. They had whiplash from looking up at the Yankees (though the 2004 postseason proved to be a marvelous cure).

The national media frequently refers to the Yankees–Red Sox rivalry as the most intense and spirited in all sports, the baseball equivalent of a Balkan dispute or a Michael Douglas divorce. The rivalry is undeniably heated—it prompted a seventy-two-year-old man who allegedly has a steel plate in his head to attack a man half his age in 2003—but true rivals are as similar as Betty and Veronica. Despite all the media hype and the 2004 championship series, the reality is that the Yankees and Red Sox most often have been as similar as the Quaid brothers.

The Red Sox have been to the World Series five times since selling Ruth to the Yankees and have won only once while the Yankees—as they are only too happy to tell you—have been to the series thirty-nine times, winning twenty-six. Until recently, one team has rarely been a factor in the other's title hopes. While New York was building its dynasty in the 1920s and '30s, Boston was finishing in last place or next-to-last eleven times. After a brief and bitter feud immediately following World War II, the two went from 1951 to 1976 without ever finishing within ten games of each other in the same season that one of them won a title.

In other words, for a quarter century, the Yankees and Red Sox played about as many meaningful games against each other in September as the Celtics and the Knicks did.

In the first forty-six years after the Ruth trade, Boston finished ahead of New York exactly twice. In four of the five seasons the Red Sox have won the pennant since 1920 the Yankees were a virtual non-entity, finishing an average of fourteen games back.

And those few times there was something on the line? Every time the poor Red Sox arrived in New York for their pennant drives, they found Travis Bickle at the wheel of their cab, running red lights, knocking over fruit stands and taking the longest route. In 1949, the Red Sox needed only to win one of the season's final two games against the Yankees. Naturally, they lost them both in a finish so epochal David Halberstam wrote a bestseller about it forty years later. In 1978, the Red Sox led the Yankees by fourteen games at one point only to blow the lead—their collapse was exemplified by the Boston Massacre that September when the Yankees swept a three-game series and outscored them 42–9—to force a one-game playoff at the end of the season. They lost that as well on the infamous Bucky Dent

home run, a defeat so devastating that it, too, sparked a bestseller—
Stephen King's *The Shining*.

Ha! Just joking. *The Shining* is about the caretaker of a mountain
lodge who is haunted by ghosts, taken over by the building's evil presence, goes steadily insane and tries to slaughter his family during the
dead of winter. The 1978 Red Sox story took place in the summer.

King did write a novel about the Red Sox, *The Girl Who Loved
Tom Gordon*. Now, when the Yankees inspire books and movies, we
get *Pride of the Yankees* and *61**, loving, sentimental propaganda
that indoctrinates new generations of fans to the New York cause and
leaves lumps in the throats of viewers so large it was as if they had
swallowed one of the Mick's empty beer bottles.

So what happened when King wrote his novel titled after the Red
Sox reliever? Gordon immediately blew out his arm and didn't save
another game for two years until he was on another team.

And then he joined the Yankees.

No wonder Sox fans can be so insane. Asked to explain the fundamental difference between Sox fans and Yankees fans, Yankeeshater
.com's Moorby replied it was a simple one. "It's 'How can we manage
to blow this game?' versus 'How can we find a way to win it?' "

Moorby, of course, said that prior to the 2004 championship series, back when a typical conversation between a Red Sox fan and a
Yankees fan still went something like this:

*Red Sox fan: "The biggest problem with Yankees fans is you're
spoiled rotten. You've won too many times to really enjoy a championship. The champagne of victory never tastes so sweet until you've
choked on the vomit of defeat while hugging the toilet in the bath-
room of the Cask 'n Flagon at three in the morning."*

Yankees fan: "Nineteen-eighteen."

*Red Sox fan: "The Yankees spend so much money that anything
less than a championship is a letdown. You'll never know the thrill
that comes with overcoming impossible odds to snatch the ultimate
prize. To appreciate winning, you first have to know the agony of being rushed to the hospital with a 104-degree fever after getting in-*

fected from a nonsterile needle while having 'Steinbrenner sucks' tattooed on your rear end."

Yankees fan: "Bucky Dent."

Red Sox fan: "Actually, I feel sorry for you. I really do. People who've never known unrequited love can never truly appreciate love. You have to know what it's like to have brain cancer slowly eat into your brain cells after using a lead-based face paint for an entire eighty-one-game home schedule, plus spring training and the post-season."

Yankees fan: "Bill Buckner."

Red Sox fan: "All right, that does it. I've had it with you. Shut your @#&%@-ing piehole!"

Yankees fan: "Roger Clemens."

Red Sox fan: "Jeter sucks!"

Yankees fan: "Grady Little."

Red Sox fan: "A-Rod swallows!!!"

Yankees fan: "Aaron Boone!"

Red Sox fan: "@#$& you!"

The conversaton usually broke down from there.

Fodor's Guide to Red Sox Nation

Red Sox Nation is a democratic country ruled by extreme baseball fundamentalists who have strict moral codes regarding everything from food (Fenway franks and clam chowda must be served before a meal can be considered kosher) to clothing. Neither women nor men may appear in public unless their heads are covered with a fitted Boston cap, strict orthodox fans must wear a Red Sox replica jersey and cannot trim their hair or shave on high holy days between April and October and pinstripes are strictly forbidden.

Sadly, this once vibrant country renowned for its exceptional universities and plentiful pubs was ravaged by an eighty-five-year war with the bordering Union of Steinbrenner Satanic Republics. The war, begun in 1920 in a dispute over the permanent residence of the Sultan of Swat, recently escalated when Red Sox Nation president Larry Lucchino called for a jihad against the decadent USSR and placed a fatwa on its despot ruler. The border between the two countries is heavily guarded and strewn with landmines, barbed wire and Big Dig contruction signs.

The war doomed generations to an endless cycle of depression and alcoholism. Formerly among the most literate countries in the world, Red Sox Nation was reduced to the home of superstitious fans who believed in ancient curses, ghosts and a progressive taxation system. Thanks, however, to its remarkable victory in the famous "Who's Your Daddy?" battle of 2004—fought over the true lineage of the royal families—the country is enjoying a staggeringly swift return to pride and prosperity.

The official currency is the Red Sox ticket, which at press time had a listed exchange rate of approximately $50 U.S. per ticket (though the black market rate was much higher). The official language is similar to English but is spoken with a thick accent that is almost unintelligible at times. "C'mon Millah, pahk it heah!" for instance, may sound like gibberish to the unfamiliar ear but they're actually saying, "Now is the winter of our discontent made glorious summer by this sun burning New York."

The language is also filled with phrases that carry multiple meanings. Depending on the context, hand gestures and time of year, "The Yankees suck," for example, can mean anything from "Good morning" to "I told you we should have got here earlier— the line outside the Cask 'n Flagon is wicked long" to "I'm going to get a shotgun and kill every damned Yankee I see."

Visitors to Red Sox Nation must first obtain a visa, tetanus shot and a "Jeter sucks!" T-shirt before clearing customs.

But Now It's Getting Personal

It is in the past decade—when the Yankees returned to the postseason after their too-short hiatus from 1982–94—that the rivalry provoked the fans into such a wild state, they all should be sporting Damon's Caveman hair style.

Fueling the emotions was Clemens's departure from Boston in 1997 followed by his trade to the Yankees in 1999. First, general manager Dan Duquette made one of the biggest blunders in front-office history by saying Clemens was over-the-hill. Well, Duquette had a point. Clemens was thirty-four and had been barely a .500 pitcher while missing almost thirty starts the previous four seasons. But he might as well have called Clemens's mother a prostitute because that was just the sort of comment bound to inspire the Rocket. Sure enough, Clemens signed with the Toronto Blue Jays and won the Cy Young the next two seasons.

Worse though, Clemens then demanded to be traded to the Yankees after their 1998 world championship season. Clemens leaving for Toronto was bad enough but to then put on the hated Yankees pinstripes? It was like Colin Powell running guns to Saddam's loyalists.

Not only did Clemens win seventy-seven games, two World Series rings and another Cy Young in New York, he spoke so often about the glories of the Yankees that he should have had his own show on the YES Network. He even said he wanted to go into Cooperstown wearing a Yankees cap even though he had pitched and won twice as many games in a Red Sox uniform. (On the other hand, since the Red Sox fired Duquette and won the 2004 World Series, Clemens now says he's willing to drop the plan to wear a "1918" T-shirt on his plaque.)

The Clemens betrayal, however, was only the appetizer in an All-U-Can-Eat menu of horror that not even King could imagine.

Both teams made the playoffs in 1995 and 1998, but they didn't meet in the postseason until the 1999 championship series when the Yankees whipped Boston in five games. A couple of horrendous umpire calls helped New York to two of the victories, and after the second one left the Red Sox trailing 3–1 in the series, enraged fans showered the field with so much garbage that you would have thought they were playing in Yankee Stadium.

While the Yankees went on to the World Series that year and the next two as well, the Red Sox could only sulk while missing the postseason the following three years. The frustration boiled over during the 2002 offseason when the Red Sox pursued Cuban defector Jose Contreras, only to have Steinbrenner decide that he couldn't tolerate Boston enjoying even this questionable minor victory. So a week after signing Japan's Hideki Matsui to a three-year, $21 million contract, the Yankees signed Contreras to a four-year $32 million contract that blew the Red Sox out of the negotiations.

The Red Sox were so upset about losing Contreras to New York, you would have thought someone had tried to cut off beer sales at Fenway. "The evil empire extends its tentacles even into Latin America," Red Sox president Larry Lucchino complained, raising the level of hyperbole to the height of the Prudential Building.

Those words, the most inspiring since John Belushi roused his Delta House brothers with the "Was it over when the Germans bombed Pearl Harbor?" speech, set the tone for the fifty-two games the two teams played against each other the next two seasons, including the infamous 2003 championship series and the much more enjoyable 2004 series.

That 2003 series was baseball's version of *Jerry Springer*. Pedro threw at Karim Garcia's head and threatened to throw at Jorge Posada's. Manny took offense at an inside pitch from Clemens and began stalking to the mound. Both benches and bullpens cleared for a brawl. Zimmer attacked Pedro, who threw him to the ground. Zimmer left in an ambulance. Garcia and Jeff Nelson got into a fight with a special-ed teacher working in the New York bullpen.

And that was just in Game 3.

The game neither team will forget was the seventh and final one when the Red Sox blew a four-run lead and Grady Little's brain suddenly turned as cold as Ted Williams's head. Little inexplicably left an obviously tired Pedro on the mound to give up seven hits to the final nine batters he faced. The eventual 6–5 loss on Boone's walk-off homer so devastated Red Sox fans that one-third of Boston TV sets still remain without screens.

The loss also cost Grady his job while ratcheting up emotions, prompting the Red Sox to gear up for the next season by trying to trade Ramirez for A-Rod over the winter. They almost pulled off the trade before getting skittish about the amount of Manny's salary Texas wanted them to pay. Not only did the trade fall apart, it backfired when the Yankees traded for Rodriguez barely a month later, adding the league's best player to their lineup—and at virtually no increase to team payroll thanks to the Rangers picking up $67 million of A-Rod's contract.

"There is really no other fair way to deal with a team that has gone so insanely far beyond the resources of all the other teams," Red Sox owner John Henry complained in an e-mail to reporters. "It will suffice to say that we have a spending limit and the Yankees apparently don't. Baseball doesn't have an answer for the Yankees."

Maybe not, but Steinbrenner had an answer for the Red Sox: *Nyah, nyah-nyah, nyah-nyah, nyah.*

"We understand that John Henry must be embarrassed, frustrated and disappointed by his failure in this transaction," Steinbrenner said in a statement. "It is time to get on with life and forget the sour grapes." George then went on the Letterman show to read off the "Top 10 Reasons It's Good to Be a Yankee," including the No. 1 reason: "You think this A-Rod deal is good, huh—we're about to sign Ty Cobb."

Henry responded to those insults by dropping his pants in the middle of Kenmore Square and telling Steinbrenner to kiss his ass. Well, to be completely honest, that didn't quite happen. Henry no doubt wanted to but he never had the chance because while he was still fiddling with his belt buckle, commissioner Bud Selig stepped in and ordered the two to knock off the bickering, shake hands and begin behaving like baseball owners are supposed to behave—by cooking their books and threatening to move out of town unless the public builds them a new $400 million stadium.

The killjoy. The beauty of a great sports rivalry is that it allows otherwise intelligent, mature people to act like fraternity boys during rush week. The whole point of letting a rivalry get overheated is that it allows us to take a break from filling out Bill Lumbergh's stupid TPS reports and feel honest-to-God passion for a night without having to buy a copy of *Maxim* magazine first. Rivalries give us an excuse to spend $250 on an officially licensed replica jersey, show up to the game in a rainbow wig while holding up a "Jeter .316" sign and egg the opposing team's bus when they leave the ballpark.

And if Giuliani is suddenly prohibited from doing that, what are the normal fans supposed to do? It's not like you can return face paint to the store after you've opened it.

The Comeback

Which brings us to 2004, the season for which Dybala and friends prepared by camping out for the first spring training game. They weren't disappointed.

Oh, the plot went in typical fashion for quite a while. The Red Sox won a bunch of games from the Yankees in April when they didn't really matter much and the Yankees won a bunch more later on when they did. They won the division for the seventh consecutive season and beat Pedro so convincingly in late September that he said in frustration, "The Yankees are my daddies."

Yankees fans were delighted, with unlicensed "Who's Your Daddy?" T-shirts soon topping such bestselling iconic New York souvenirs as Statue of Liberty figurines, "I ♥ New York" shirts and $20 Rolex watches. It also set the stage for a championship series so compelling that you expected to see it featured on not only the cover of *Sports Illustrated* and *ESPN the Magazine* but also the *National Enquirer* ("Johnny Damon Is Matt and Ben's Love Child!"). Demand for tickets was so high that the Kennedy family probably scalped tickets outside the stadium.

With New York fans chanting "Who's Your Daddy?" so often that it was like being at Shawn Kemp's Father's Day picnic, the Yankees won the first two games at Yankee Stadium, then routed the Red Sox 19–8 in Game 3 at Fenway. But then something strange and wonderful happened.

With the Yankees just three outs from sweeping the series, Mariano Rivera on the mound and Boston fans wondering whether to leap from the top of the Citgo sign or into the Charles River, the Red Sox stormed back. They beat the Yankees 6–4 in twelve innings in Game 4. They beat them 5–4 in Game 5 the next night in fourteen innings. They went back to New York and beat them 4–2 in Game 6 to force a final game. All of a sudden, it was the Red Sox who were tallying back in the final inning and the Yankees who had turned into Team Heimlich.

The Yankees attempted to invoke the old ghosts before Game 7 by having Bucky Dent throw out the ceremonial first pitch to Yogi, but it didn't work. The Red Sox scored two runs in the first inning, four more in the second and whipped them 10–3 to clinch the pennant and finally crush their nemesis.

It was the most uplifting, unifying moment in Boston sports since Norm, Cliff and Woody stole Wade Boggs's pants on *Cheers*. As one Red Sox fan shouted after one of the victories, "I'm going to dance in the street and hug strangers!"

"Tonight is about winning the American League and going through the Yankees to do it," champagne-soaked Boston general manager Theo Epstein said after Game 7. "This is for all the great Red Sox teams and players that would have been in the World Series if it hadn't been for the Yankees. The 1949 team, 1978, 1999, last year.

"This is for all the fans who would have been able to go to the World Series if it hadn't been for the Yankees."

Indeed, the series had a profound effect on the fans. Like a shaggy Saddam Hussein pulled from a spider hole, the defeated Yankees no longer seemed quite so menacing a villain. *Boston Globe* cartoonist Dan Wasserman drew a panel showing a boy dressed up as a Yankee for Halloween. "Ah, that doesn't scare anyone," his friend tells him.

Suddenly, it was as if the Red Sox were wearing pinstripes. The Red Sox not only went on to win the World Series, they did it in almost Yankee-like fashion, leading in every single inning en route to a convincing sweep over the Cardinals. Fans throughout New England were so excited that the victory parade outdrew the annual kegger at the Kennedy compound. "The best part of this is all those Red Sox fans don't have anything to be upset about anymore," first baseman Doug Mientkiewicz said. "They don't have to be depressed and wait for something bad to happen. They can smile and be happy."

Will they? New England fans had been asking themselves since before construction began on the Big Dig how good it would feel to finally win a World Series. And now that they have, will it be as satisfying as they expect? Will the joy prove longer-lasting than the permanent in Pedro's hair? Will they truly reverse the curse and repeatedly win at New York's expense? Or will the loss of the distinctive part of their character leave them as just another boring faceless ballclub like the Baltimore Orioles or the Anaheim Angels?

Time will tell. But whatever happens, like Bogie and Paris, at least they'll always have the Yankees.

Yankees fan: *"All right, so you finally won one series against us when it actually meant something. Now get over yourselves."*

Red Sox fan: *"Who's your Papi!!!"*

Yankees fan: *"Actually, I think it's kind of nice that you won, I really do. At least now we don't have to hear your pathetic whining about how much you suffered over all those years. Doris Kearns Goodwin and Stephen King should finally be happy."*

Red Sox fan: *"David Ortiz!"*

Yankees fan: *"I mean, it's not like this changes anything. We've still won twenty-six championships since 1918 and you've still only won one and we're still going to kick your ass again next year. You do know that, don't you?"*

Red Sox fan: *"Kevin Brown!"*

Yankees fan: *"All right, that does it. I've had it with you. Shut your @#&%@-ing piehole!"*

Red Sox fan: *"A-Fraud!"*

Yankees fan: "Schilling sucks!"
Red Sox fan: "Jeter swallows!"
Yankees fan: "@#$& you!"
Red Sox fan: "@#$& you!"
Yankees fan: "No, @#$& you!"
Red Sox fan: "No, @#$& you!"

See? There still *are* some things you can rely on in this world.

The Alternate World

We all know that the Red Sox sold Babe Ruth to the Yankees before the 1920 season, turning New York into baseball's ruling dynasty. At least that's what happened in *our* world. But there is an alternate world that was identical to ours except for one key difference—in the alternate world, Boston kept Ruth. And that one decision had a profound effect on history.

Some of the key ways the alternate world differs from ours:

Ted Williams is still alive, unfrozen and known by his nickname, "Mr. October."

Joe DiMaggio is still alive and known only as "Mr. Monroe."

Based on the insufferable yearly championships of baseball's most hated team, the longest-running musical in Broadway history is still running after fifty-one years: *Damn Cubbies.*

The Dodgers are still in Brooklyn but the Yankees moved to Los Angeles and changed their name to the Migrant Workers.

Lee Harvey Oswald missed.

There is no designated hitter or artificial turf.

John Lennon never met Yoko and the Beatles stayed together.

Mickey Mantle lived and is the director emeritus of Alcoholics Anonymous.

George Steinbrenner was fired after losing his ship company in a hostile takeover and now works as a greeter at a Wal-Mart in Conneaut, Ohio.

Betamax became the video recording standard. Apple software triumphed over Microsoft. Everyone loved New Coke.

Hall of Famer Bill Buckner made a brilliant diving stop on Mookie Wilson's roller down the first base line to complete Boston's twenty-fifth world championship.

Pete Rose never bet on baseball.

Sated by Boston's many championships, Red Sox fanatic Ben Affleck never made a movie.

Roger Clemens has pitched his entire career with the Red Sox and performs his famous ritual before each start when he rubs the nose of the Babe Ruth plaque, which is right between the Mantle, Gehrig and Jackie Robinson plaques in Fenway's Monument Park.

Clay beat Ruben on *American Idol.*

 ## *The Babe Comes Clean*

"Look, can we finally put this curse nonsense to rest? There was never any damn Curse of the Bambino. I don't know how I can put it any simpler. THERE WAS NEVER A CURSE!!!! Good Lord. It was just a book written more than four decades after I died and some editor in Manhattan probably thought up the title one day after having a couple of extra martinis at lunch. It was never meant to be taken literally.

"It's like the travel guys who put out those books, *New York City on $40 a Day.* You can't even park a car in New York for $40 a day unless you want your hubcaps stolen during the game. It's just a title to grab your attention and make you pick it up off the shelf, like that *Naked Chicks with Big Jugs* magazine Lou Gehrig used to keep hidden in the back of his locker that he didn't think any of us knew about. And yet people swallow that curse thing like it came straight from the Holy Bible. It's sad.

"Why would I place a curse on the Red Sox anyway? Harry Hooper, Everett Scott, Stuffy McInnis—I loved those guys. I wanted nothing but success for them. Though, I wish I could find out who smeared peanut butter in my underwear that one time in Cleveland. And why would I want to keep Boston's fans from enjoying a championship? Those fans were always great to me. I never had a bartender or a woman turn me down in that town.

"If I wanted to place a real curse on someone, believe me, I would have—beginning with those no-good owners. And I'm not talking just Boston's Harry Frazee for selling me to New York. I'd also have put a hex on that cheap bastard, Jacob Ruppert, for cutting my salary practically in half in 1934 after I hit thirty-four home runs. And believe me, the curse would have been directed specifically at those guys, no one else. I'd have had Ruppert fall down an elevator shaft or have Frazee come down with a venereal disease. Something that would cause them as much pain as they caused us players.

"But I couldn't place a curse on them, because there are no such things as curses. Sorry to break the news, but there are no such things as ghosts, secret spells or the Evil Eye, either. Proctor and Gamble isn't owned by devil worshippers and the *Blair Witch Project* is just a movie. And voodoo doesn't work either, no matter how many roosters that moron Joe McCarthy had us sacrifice whenever we got in a deep slump. The plain and simple reason the Red Sox didn't win a World Series for all those years is they weren't good enough. End of story.

"On the other hand, there's no doubt about it—the Cubs are cursed big time."

CHAPTER 8

The Dump That Ruth Built

Other teams do a nice job promoting their past; the Yankees let you actually smell it.

While covering the first game of the 2003 playoffs between New York and Boston, I noticed a pool of vomit on one of the Yankee Stadium ramps leading to the mezzanine level. It was still there the next game, though it had dried by that point. When the series returned to New York the next week, the vomit still was there. And when the World Series began, it still was there (though some attempt apparently had been made to finally clean it). And when the World Series ended a week later, you could still see the stain.

Now, I assume the vomit was from a fan who had a little too much to drink during Game 1 of the Red Sox series. Given the general attention to cleanliness at the stadium, though, it might have been from the day Wally Pipp blew chunks and Gehrig's playing streak began. I tend to doubt it, though, because if it was, the Yankees would have put it on display in Monument Park or sold it in commemorative one-ounce vials for $29.95 at their stadium store.

While it seems from the bathrooms and overall sanitation that Yankee Stadium must have been built before modern plumbing, the team actually didn't move into the stadium until 1923, after having spent its first two decades in other locations. The Yankees played their first ten seasons at long-gone and nearly forgotten Hilltop Park in Washington Heights. The tiny ballpark had seating for 16,000 fans and took only six weeks to build, which is slightly less time that it takes to buy a hot dog these days at Yankee Stadium. The ballpark was largely financed on Tammany Hall graft and it showed—though the stadium cost what was then considered a great amount of money, it lacked grass on much of the outfield, and right field was a virtual sinkhole that occasionally had to be roped off (which, coincidentally, was often the case in the days when Reggie played in right field). In other words, even way back then, the Yankees didn't operate on a level playing field.

(It was also crooked—for a time the Yankees had a scout with a pair of binoculars in a nearby apartment house stealing signals and flashing them to the Yankees batters with a mirror.)

Transportation to the then-remote stadium was difficult, and after averaging less than 3,200 fans a game in 1912 (about 60 percent of the league average), the Yankees moved out of Hilltop to begin sharing the Polo Grounds with the Giants. It was an uneasy and often difficult relationship, much like Tom Cruise and Nicole Kidman's. Giants pitcher Christy Mathewson was a neat freak who constantly complained that Ruth always left the toilet seat up, played his Led Zeppelin albums at top volume until three in the morning and ate everyone else's food in the refrigerator without ever offering to pay for it. The arrangement lasted a decade—the two teams played the 1921 and 1922 World Series against each other at the Polo Grounds— before the Giants finally grew tired of picking up Ruth's dirty underwear and empty pizza cartons and abruptly evicted the Yankees.

(The Yankees also shared Shea Stadium with the Mets in 1974 and 1975 while Yankee Stadium was being refurbished. The Mets are still trying to find out who stuck them with all the long-distance phone calls to Los Angeles, though they suspect it was Ron Blomberg.)

While the Giants' decision was understandable, it also was one that wound up haunting every team in baseball. Kicked out of the Polo Grounds, the Yankees put Ruth to work, instructing him to build a 700,000-square-foot house across the Harlem River that would be large enough for the team to play its games. (For further details, see "The House That I Built.")

The House That I Built

"Everyone thinks 'The House That Ruth Built' refers to the huge crowds of fans I attracted, which both created the necessity for a larger stadium and generated the revenues to build one. That's inaccurate. I *really built* the stadium. No joking, it was all me, beginning with picking the site. Colonel Ruppert wanted to build it on Manhattan's Upper West Side but I talked him out of it. You want to build in the Bronx, I told him. The land will be cheap, traffic jams will be nonexistent and parking will never, ever be a problem. And the stadium will spin off so much ancillary business that the surrounding neighborhood will quickly become the city's most desirable, lined with so many quaint shops and cafes it would be known as the Paris of the Bronx.

"You know how it's 295 feet down the right-field line but was 460 feet to left center? That was no accident—I drew up the blueprints and I made sure it was a great place for a left-handed slugger. I'll admit, having had no formal education beyond the eighth grade, the blueprints weren't easy, but I got some architectural tips from the engineering department at Columbia University. That's where I first met Lou Gehrig. We would stay up late talking about the Bauhaus movement and the exciting things Frank Lloyd Wright was doing with concrete reinforcement. The club originally signed him to help me engineer the sewer and electrical lines; that he could play first base and hit like Jimmie Foxx was just a bonus.

"We broke ground in 1922 and finished in 284 days, but it would have gone a lot quicker had I not been playing ball from April to October. Fortunately, the Yankees played right across the river at the Polo Grounds, so after the games I would just put on my hard hat and walk across the bridge to work on the stadium until it got too dark. It was tiring work but it helped me as a player. Jeff Kent is wrong—I didn't take steroids, because I never needed them. Swinging crowbars and laying girder made me so strong that a fifty-four-ounce Louisville Slugger felt like nothing.

"Of course, I didn't build it *all by myself*. I hired some of those Mohawk ironworkers for the high beam work. And teammates helped out from time to time, except for that lazy Wally Pipp. That's the real reason he called in sick that day—he just wanted to get out of pulling his shift on the rivet detail.

"But mostly, that's my baby. It wasn't bad for a first project but I'm prouder of my later works. Now, the Chrysler Building—I could tell you some stories."

The original Yankee Stadium was one of baseball's true palaces. The first baseball ballpark to be called a stadium, it towered over the surrounding neighborhood and was so gigantic that no one ever hit a home run beyond its walls. This genuinely historic park had grandeur (there were 80,000 seats at one point), charming detail (the monuments to Ruth, Gehrig and Miller Huggins were in play in center field) and architectural elegance (the copper frieze lining the upper deck was as treasured a part of Yankees lore as the pinstripes on DiMaggio's uniform or the mustard stains on Ruth's). The Babe may not have actually built the stadium but it certainly was built *for* him—the right-field corner was an inviting 295 feet down the line for Ruth and other lefties, while DiMaggio and other right-handers could only watch as their fly balls were swallowed up by power alley in left center field that was so deep (457 feet from home plate) that were the park still that large, George W. Bush would open it up for clear-cutting.

Many of baseball's most memorable and cherished moments occurred within its walls: Ruth's mammoth home runs, Gehrig's farewell speech, the beginning of DiMaggio's hitting streak, Don Larsen's perfect game in the 1956 World Series, Maris's sixty-first home run and, of course, all those World Series games. The stadium also was the site of epic football games between Notre Dame and Army, world championship fights, the famous 1958 NFL title game between the Giants and Colts, and even a papal visit. Everyone who was anyone played at old Yankee Stadium, except for the Beatles, who instead chose Shea Stadium for their 1965 U.S. tour in what was their most inexplicable move outside the lyrics to "I Am the Walrus."

Unfortunately, Steinbrenner and company corrupted that history with the notorious remodeling after the 1973 season. Death Valley was moved in, the monuments were moved out, two-thirds of the least-expensive seats in the bleachers were removed and the historic copper trim largely disappeared (replaced with plastic) along with much of the stadium's charm. It was as if someone had decided to remodel the Chrysler Building by first removing the hood ornament gargoyles.

Walk into Fenway Park or Wrigley Field and you get the feeling that time has stood still for decades—literally so for Cubs fans, waiting for another world championship flag to go up the pole. They are genuinely *parks*. There have been substantial changes to both over the years, but they all have been made carefully enough to preserve the original structure to the point that you can practically see Ted Williams and Hack Wilson popping up in the clutch. Although both have their faults (for one thing, tickets are so expensive that the only people who can afford them are the players themselves), Fenway and Wrigley are our nation's own little Wayback Machines, with Sherman and Mr. Peabody transporting us back to what baseball was like when our grandparents were young.

Unfortunately, the only impression you get at Yankee Stadium is that it hasn't been *cleaned since* our grandparents were young. The very bad 1993 movie *The Babe* opens with what is supposed to be a loving aerial shot of Yankee Stadium accompanied by the sounds of the crowd and the crack of Ruth's bat, but the scene doesn't work at all because today's Yankee Stadium simply doesn't look like the Yankee Stadium of the Babe's day.

Walk into Yankee Stadium and it's like walking back to 1978, except the prices are higher and the haircuts are shorter. Even the Yankees acknowledged this with a recent plan for a new stadium whose exterior would closely resemble the original.

On the other hand, the mid-'70s remodel did include a 138-foot stainless steel and fiberglass smokestack in the shape of a baseball bat that vents exhaust fumes, some of which do not originate from Steinbrenner's mouth. So, it has that going for it, which is nice.

No Wonder Yankees Fans Are So Angry All the Time

Yankee Stadium's field is as sacred a national landmark as the Alamo, Monticello or Madonna's bedroom, but the real problem is when you look away from the diamond. ESPN.com surveyed every major league ballpark in 2003, rating each on everything from architecture to the bathrooms to the price of hot dogs, and Yankee Stadium ranked twenty-first, behind the Marlins' park (and no, I did *not* rate Yankee Stadium in the survey). Little wonder. Only the ballpark's history and the great players who have called its field home make Yankee Stadium special.

 Retired Numbers

As all fans know, the Yankees have honored many players by retiring their jerseys, erecting plaques in Monument Park or even preserving their old lockers—Thurman Munson's locker was set aside so no one else would use it after his death a quarter century ago, prompting one player to comment after being traded to New York, "What, do they expect him to come back or something?"

Less known is the fact that they have also recognized many other lesser players by retiring other parts of their uniforms and/ or the clubhouse. Among the highlights:

Horace Clarke's pants

Mickey Rivers's protective cup

Joe Pepitone's toupee

Hank Bauer's underwear

Oscar Gamble's hairnet

Luis Polonia's pornography

David Wells's empties

Moose Skowron's spittoon

Bobby Murcer's remote control

Rickey Henderson's card table

Ron Blomberg's glove

Even the scoreboard is substandard. Fenway and Wrigley have notable hand-operated scoreboards displaying the scores of every out-of-town game. Their scoreboards are so beautiful that I would be willing to buy a ticket when the local team wasn't playing just to see them change the scores on the games from around the league. The Yankees, however, somehow cannot find room in their massive stadium for an out-of-town scoreboard, displaying such scores only on occasion on a small revolving electronic sign that isn't visible to everyone. The scores are shown even less now than they were in the past because the Yankees use the space to sell advertisements.

After all, when you have revenues as limited as the Yankees, you have to make the money wherever you can.

In other cities, scoreboard-watching provides tense moments when fans can see how rivals are faring in the pennant race. *Are they gaining? Are they falling behind?* Scoreboard-watching at Yankee Stadium provides tense moments when fans can see what products

Nobody Beats the Wiz has on sale. But in a way, that's fitting. After all, Yankees fans don't care that other teams are playing, so why would their glorious stadium waste precious space showing *those* scores?

Granted, the stadium is old (it was built before Bob Sheppard's voice changed). No one expects there to be brewpubs and swimming pools and petting zoos or any of the other accoutrements that are all but mandatory at new stadiums. But Kauffman (Royals) Stadium opened before Yankee Stadium's renovation and it not only is a superior park, it still looks as if it were built yesterday. Yankee Stadium looks about like what you would expect from an owner who has been trying to get the city to build him a new facility for the past decade and hasn't tipped the building super for even longer than that.

The concession stands and bathrooms are small and inadequate in number. The lines emerging from the women's rooms have been known to stretch so far that Oprah must be giving away free Pontiacs inside. There are few TV monitors to keep track of the game, while concession lines are so long that the Department of Motor Vehicles seems efficient. While other stadiums offer everything from crab and salmon sandwiches to garlic fries, plus a full array of microbrews, the Yankees don't offer much beyond hot dogs, beer, soda and coffee at most stands. The Yankees evidently figure that whatever was good enough for Fiorello La Guardia is good enough for today's fans.

The stadium concourses, meanwhile, are so narrow that walking through them is like serving on a German U-boat, only with staler air and more danger of a beam falling from the ceiling. When fans attempt to file out of the stadium following a game, they resemble a blood clot slowly forcing its way through David Wells's cholesterol-choked artery. On the plus side, though, this has the benefit of allowing the many drunk fans to be efficiently carried out with the tide.

All the while, ushers and stadium security eye fans with the sort of glare last seen on Bernie Goetz just before he reached for his gun in a subway car. Israel's elite Sayeret Matkal commando team may be considered the world's most elite fighting unit, but legend has it the majority of their recruits volunteered only after flunking out of the intense Yankee Stadium security training program.

If You Build It, He'll Make Money

Yankee Stadium is such a garbage dump that Steinbrenner has been bitching about a new stadium for years, actively discouraging fans from attending his team's games by suggesting that the surrounding Bronx neighborhood is unsafe and undesirable, traffic is a gridlock mess and parking is nonexistent.

Even though there is no chance the Yankees would ever leave the New York metropolitan area and its staggering broadcast revenues, Steinbrenner somehow convinced Giuliani, the Official Yankees Mascot, to propose the construction of an $800 million replacement (see designs) as one of his final acts before leaving the mayor's office. The $800 million was just the estimated cost, though. By the time the stadium actually would have been finished behind schedule and everyone had been properly paid off, the cost undoubtedly would have been much, much more. And this at a time when New York City was still recovering from September 11. Fortunately, when Mayor Bloomberg took office, he announced that a baseball stadium for a multimillionaire was not exactly a priority for a city that was billions of dollars in the red and facing the devastating loss of the casts from *Sex and the City* and *Friends* in the same spring.

Blocked by Bloomberg, Steinbrenner and the Yankees eventually were forced to propose another stadium plan in 2004. Realizing that no one was going to approve a stadium for the richest team in sports, the Yankees proposed building a replacement across the street from the current stadium and—in the most shocking development since the end of *The Sixth Sense*—offered to pay for the "estimated" $700 million to $750 million cost themselves. The funding plan was still a little unclear at the time of publication but it is believed to be modeled on the scheme first developed by Ralph Bellamy and Don Ameche in the 1983 movie *Trading Places*. A little-known codicil in the major league baseball constitution allows teams to deduct stadium costs from their revenue-sharing obligations, so the Yankees could issue tax-free industrial bonds and pay them off every year with

The House That Rudy Would Have Built

As one of his last acts as mayor of New York, Rudy Giuliani approved the construction of a brand-new stadium. Unfortunately for the Yankees, when incoming mayor Michael Bloomberg took office, he said there was no money. We're proud to present the plans for Rudy's dreamed-of Yankee World.

The WTC Memorial Twin Luxury Towers – 110 floors of luxury suites in each tower, each a tribute to the fallen heroes of 9/11, as well as a needed revenue stream for the Yankees.

Relive the Yankees golden era and mingle with former greats at the Copacabana. Just be careful around the animatronic Billy Martin after he's had a few belts.

It may take a little enginee but all subway tracks will to Yankee World after Gra Central Station is relocate underneath the stadium.

The finest fans in the world deserve the finest food, so Yankee World concessions will be owned and operated by Dean & Deluca. Hello, sliced foie gras de moulard!

Giuliani's extraordinary vision solves two problems at once, by getting the homeless off the street and back to work raking the infield.

RUMP CASINOS

the same money they would otherwise have to send into the revenue-sharing pool.

I've got to hand it to them—it's an ingenious plan, really. With naming rights—don't be surprised if we one day hear Bob Sheppard announcing, "Ladies and gentlemen, CEOs and heart surgeons, welcome to Utz Potato Chip Field at Halliburton Park"—the new stadium could actually cost the Yankees less than a middle reliever. And not only would the Yankees generate more revenue, they would share less of it with their fellow teams.

Of course, the city and state still would be on the hook for staggering infrastructure costs, including parks and public transportation. Those are the sort of improvements that owners always claim are needed to spur business in the surrounding neighborhoods, but Yankee Stadium is proof that this often isn't the case, unless you count the scalpers lining the sidewalks in groups so thick they outnumber even the homeless urinating under the 161st Street subway stop. Apart from the McDonald's, the most visible nearby business is Stan's Baseball Land, a souvenir shop with a name straight out of a Moroccan bazaar, where one imagines fans bartering with hookah-smoking merchants.

"How much for the Yankees cap?"

"Ah, I can see that you are a devout fan of the great and glorious Bronx Bombers. For you, a special bargain. Only thirty dollars."

"Thirty bucks? That's outrageous. The guys in the stadium charge less than that."

"You insult me, you son of a goat! Examine the cap for yourself. See the exquisite, painstaking craftsmanship. We use only the finest wool from sheep raised in our own apartment. Truly, the odor is oppressive and my son has been tempted into unspeakable acts of perversion. My daughter personally hand-sews the logo on the caps from morning to nightfall until her fingers are raw and bleed scarlet rivers. I fear no man will take her as a wife. And you dare compare the quality of these caps to the ones sold in the stadium? You are lucky I do not call for the elders to have you shackled and flogged until the flesh peels from your

back, but instead I will take twenty-five dollars just to rid you from my store!"

"I'll give you twenty dollars."

"Done. And could I interest you in an A-Rod replica jersey?"

Still, in an age when most owners' stadium-financing proposals usually involve Luca Brasi and a severed horse head, the Yankees deserve some credit for paying a large share of the costs.

But what would become of current Yankee Stadium if a replacement is indeed built? What would become of the stadium where the Babe, Gehrig, Joltin' Joe, the Mick, Reggie and Jeter won pennant after pennant and thrilled fans for generations? What would become of one of the most historic structures in all baseball?

Early plans called for turning the House That Ruth Built into a parking structure. And the worst part of that is you know it will always be filled, so that you still wind up paying $30 for a spot on the street that some guy swears will be safe; but when you come back after the game someone will not only have stolen your Minnesota Twins antennae ball, they'll have broken the antennae off and used it to hot-wire your car and leave you stranded in the Bronx at midnight.

Arrgghhh! When am I ever going to learn!

CHAPTER 9

Yank-Jazeera

Philo T. Farnsworth had high hopes for television when he invented it, dreaming that it would dramatically change the world by educating and connecting people around the globe. By the mid-1950s, however, he was so appalled by the direction television had taken and its effects on society that when panelists on the *I've Got a Secret* game show asked whether his invention was a machine that caused pain, he replied, "Yes, sometimes it's most painful."

"I suppose you could say that he felt he had created kind of a monster, a way for people to waste a lot of their lives," Farnsworth's son once said, adding, "Throughout my childhood his reaction to television was 'There's nothing on it worthwhile.' "

And remember, Farnsworth felt that way even though he died more than thirty years before the first episode of *Yankeeography* debuted on the YES Network.

The YES Network, or as some of us like to call it, Yank-Jazeera, combines two of the most dreaded elements in American society— the Yankees and a cable TV operator—into a single grotesque entity that represents the gravest threat to television viewers since Terry Bradshaw sang "A Hard Day's Night" with Paul McCartney during the Super Bowl. Yank-Jazeera presents a 24/7 look at baseball that is "fair and balanced" in the same way as Fox News. The only thing missing from their broadcasts is former Iraqi information minister Muhammad Saeed al-Sahaf providing the late-night highlights.

"The brilliant tactician Joe Torre drew the imperial Boston invaders into a master trap on the sacred soil of Yankee Stadium and then tightened the noose tonight in the Mother of All Games! The heroic Derek Jeter drove the criminal Pedro Martinez's pitiful fastballs out of the stadium and across our sovereign border with tape-measure home runs that are still in flight! The brave Yankee fielders caught the ridiculous Red Sox fly balls as if they were fish in the river! The corrupt Boston mercenaries are trapped in the mud and the valiant Yankee Guard shall chop them up and throw them back into the sea! Steinbrenner is good! All praise Torre! Back to you, Fred!"

"Actually, Muhammad, the Yankees lost 4–1."

In Stanley Kubrick's movie *A Clockwork Orange*, government officials inject Malcolm McDowell with a serum that induces nausea, strap him into a chair with a straitjacket, clamp his eyelids open and force him to watch an endless stream of violent movie sequences. It could have been worse. They could have made him sit through twenty-four hours of Yank-Jazeera. Trust me. I know. I did one day in what I look back upon as my own personal Vietnam.

All Yankees, All the Time

6:30 p.m. My broadcast day begins with the half-hour Yankees pregame show, which gives a rundown on starting pitchers, injuries and trade rumors. Fred Hickman does a good job, as do reporter Suzyn Waldman and broadcasters Michael Kay, Ken Singleton and Joe Girardi. Maybe this marathon won't be so bad, after all.

7:00 p.m. The Yankees–Blue Jays game from SkyDome. Sure, the YES broadcasters are unapologetic homers, but which team's aren't? Broadcast teams are as inherently biased as Bill O'Reilly—it's just part of the gig. And aside from the predictable Yankees bombast, the YES broadcast is quite good. The production standards are first-rate, there are plenty of camera angles and Girardi provides some insightful analysis. And remember, this was on a night when Jim Kaat (one of the best in the business) wasn't working.

No, I have only one real complaint with the broadcast. The Yankees rally from a 2–1 deficit and win.

10:45 p.m. The Yankees postgame show. We get highlights from the win, comments from Torre and much hand-wringing over the Yankees' frail starting pitching. Typical. The Yankees win and they bitch that they didn't win easily enough. Still, if the YES Network can fill the rest of my broadcast schedule like this with games and analysis, it could be an enjoyable day.

Unfortunately, the next offering is *Yankeeography*.

Tonight's restrained episode details Derek Jeter's life story, from his birth in a manger in Kalamazoo, Michigan, to his glories in the Bronx. "Is it possible to be any cooler than Derek Jeter?" host John Sterling asks with the tone of an anchorman at a state funeral. "Smart, single, good-looking, on the cover of *GQ*, host of *Saturday Night Live*. . . . You couldn't ask for a better man to serve as [the team's] leader—than Derek."

Wow, John. Nice job. Would you like to smoke a cigarette now?

12:15 a.m. *Yankees Encore.* A replay of the night's Blue Jays game. Okay, this is not exactly what I wanted to see right away again—where, oh where is "Beck's CenterStage with Michael Kay" that I keep seeing promos for?—but it goes by painlessly enough thanks to several innings being edited out. Unfortunately, those deleted innings do not include the Yankees' winning rally.

1:28 a.m. Am I getting sleepy, or did I just see a promo for an upcoming episode of *Yankees Classic,* showing a replay of a game from *May*?

1:49 a.m. No, I was right. The promo just came on again.

3:00 a.m. Naturally, even a network devoted to the great Yankees cannot fill twenty-four entire hours with original programming. So YES fills the late-night slots with the broadcast offerings that everyone pays $70 a month in cable fees to watch: infomercials. On the one hand, it's refreshing to get a break from the relentless Yankees propaganda—there is no infomercial for "Jeter Girls Gone Wild"—but it's enough to make me pine for a nice Monster Truck rerun. Let's see. There is "Six-Second Abs," "The Secrets to Real Estate Success," "Urban Rebounding" fitness equipment and "Body by Jake" fitness videos. There also is an infomercial for a unique germ-free toothbrush, which claims that the toothbrush is a more important invention than the computer, the car or television.

I'm not sure about the car and the computer, but as the sun rises over the horizon for hour eleven of my YES marathon, I'm inclined to agree that TV might be overrated.

3:27 a.m. Arrgggghhh!!! Reggie's commercial for the Hit-A-Way batting machine has now run so many times that I'm tempted to order the entire remaining stock just so I won't have to see this thing anymore.

4:26 a.m. Getting very, very tired. In my weakened state, I think I just ordered a YES logo sweatshirt and cap for $40, not including shipping.

6:30 a.m. *This Week in Baseball*. Wow. Thank God there's the YES Network. Otherwise, where would anyone ever be able to watch this show, which is broadcast every week over free TV in every market in the country?

7:00 a.m. *Kids on Deck*, a thirty-minute show for younger fans, who apparently enjoy seeing Hillary Duff in a Yankees jersey explaining that hitting .300 with thirty home runs is really, really good. Willie Randolph also shows kids what the clubhouse lounge looks like, telling them that the Yankees' favorite movie is *Tombstone*, a movie that doesn't seem to have nearly enough nudity or fart jokes to really be that popular with big league ballplayers.

I guess the good news is Luis Polonia is nowhere near the set.

7:30 a.m. *What's It Worth?* An *Antiques Roadshow* for sports fans, with collectors bringing in their Yankees memorabilia for appraisal from John Brigandi and host Andrea Joyce. Sadly, Ruben Rivera's "secret" collection is not assessed.

8:00 a.m. *Yankees Network Magazine.* Am I dreaming now or did this half-hour show actually open with host Leslie Boghosian taking her dog to a yoga class? Whatever, this is followed by a report on a man who claims there are sixteen major brain types, and most great athletes have the same one, including A-Rod. There is no video, however, of this guy reading the bumps on Zimmer's noggin.

8:30 a.m. *Running.* A half-hour show on the recent women's mini-10K in Central Park and the 1989 Cascade Runoff in Portland, Oregon. This is a puzzling programming choice. Having spent a night in the Yankee Stadium bleachers, I can't believe there is a large crossover in Yankees fans and running enthusiasts.

9:00 a.m. Just what I needed after a sleepless night and nearly sixteen hours of YES programming. Another encore presentation of last night's game. Unfortunately, the Yankees still win.

11:30 a.m. Oh, joy! Oh, rapture! It's time for more *Yankeeography!* This episode's subject: Willie Randolph. "Throughout his thirteen years as a second baseman and more than a decade as a coach," Sterling says with the tone James Earl Jones used in his baseball speech in *Field of Dreams*, "Willie Randolph has been a champion of the Yankees way. Consistent, hardworking, dependable . . . a *winner*."

Quick, where's the official YES logo barf bag?

12:30 p.m. *Yankees Magazine.* I was hoping this would be a replay from the 8 a.m. show so I could nod off for a while, but it's not. The morning show was *Yankees Network Magazine.* This is *Yankees Magazine*, a weekly roundup of the club's games and news, including more testimonials to pinstripe greatness from Moose Skowron and Jim Leyritz ("I will forever be a Yankee. No matter what I do, I will be tied to this organization," says Leyritz, who meant so little to the Yankees that they traded him for two players to be named later) and a segment on how great the Yankees are at coming from behind to win games. "It's amazing," infielder Miguel Cairo says. "When [teams] play us, they have to get twenty-seven outs."

As opposed to other teams, I guess, who apparently call it a night and go home sometime in the eighth inning.

1:00 p.m. *Mike and the Mad Dog* simulcast. Look, *listening* to sports talk radio is grueling enough. I cannot think of a duller, drearier way to spend an afternoon than by *watching* talk radio on TV for two hours.

Unfortunately, the simulcast lasts five and a half hours.

2:43 p.m. The YES Network finally gets around to showing Aaron Boone's 2003 winning home run as one of its "Classic Moments," twenty hours after I first turned on the TV. Undoubtedly, someone will be fired for this oversight.

4:36 p.m. I give up! I know there are only two hours left but I can't take it anymore. I not only want to turn off the TV, I want to kick in the screen and call the FCC to demand that they shoot the YES Network's satellite out of its orbit.

But if I do that, I won't be able to watch "Best of Mike and the Mad Dog" when it airs at 10:30, right after the game and before.

The Medium Is the Message

Yank-Jazeera is merely the latest Ballantine Blast in New York's lucrative broadcasting history, which dates back to when Mel Allen was doing play-by-play with tin cans and a really long string.

The Pittsburgh Pirates were the first team to broadcast their games on radio, in 1921, with KDKA's Harold Arlin coining the phrase "The windup and the pitch." (I think his descendants still receive royalty checks every month.) Other teams followed, but even as radio's popularity exploded across the country, the Yankees remained suspicious of the new medium. In 1932, they and the two other New York clubs declared an informal city radio blackout in fear that fans would stop buying tickets if they could stay home and listen to the games for free. This was an extremely shortsighted view—broadcasts actually spur ticket sales through increased interest—but remember, the Yankees have a genetic aversion to giving away anything for free. Then-Dodgers club president Larry MacPhail lifted the Cone of Silence on New York in 1938, and the Yankees responded the next season by putting a microphone in front of the man whose voice millions of Americans would soon grow to trust for his stirring daily reports, gathering by their radios to listen to his still-famous signature line: "This . . . is London."

Just kidding. That was Edward R. Murrow's signature line and he delivered it each night during the Blitz from the London rooftops, where he had fled to escape the range of the Yankees radio broadcasts. Back home in New York, Mel Allen was delivering his signature line, "How about that!" (which, according to radio legend, he chose only after the censors rejected his proposed "Shit, did you see that?"). Those first Yankees broadcasts forever changed baseball and life in general. No longer were citizens able to avoid the Yankees by simply staying away from the Bronx; suddenly you weren't safe from hearing someone gush over the team even while sitting in the privacy of your living room.

"Fans, I wish you could see with your own eyes just how inspiring these Yankees are. I tell you, when so much of society outside Yankee Stadium seems to be falling apart, it makes you proud to be an American when you know there are fine, upstanding young men in pinstripes who still represent everything that is good and decent in this country of ours. And now, here's Joe DiMaggio with a brief word from our sponsors."

"Thanks, Mel. You know, kids, it can get pretty nerve-wracking before a big game, but nothing relaxes me like the cool menthol flavor of a Chesterfield cigarette. Plus, they really help keep the weight off. But when I'm trying to wind down after another exciting victory and a three-for-five day at the plate, nothing beats a refreshing Ballantine beer."

The broadcasts not only brought the Yankees into our homes as unwelcome guests (Lefty Gomez never bothered to flush the toilet), they gave the team the PIN number to the sporting world's richest ATM.

Having overcome their fears of radio, the Yankees became the first major league team to sign a local television contract by selling their rights in 1946 for $75,000. That doesn't sound like much, but remember, their Nielsen ratings were still pretty low in 1946 because virtually the only person who could afford to own one of the few televisions in use was playing center field for the Yankees.

As the ownership of TV sets grew, so did the broadcasting revenue, climbing to $2 million a year in 1964, or enough to cover the team payroll, plus the bar tab for Mantle and Ford at Toots Shor's. The revenue and programming possibilities for the game's most successful team in its largest market had grown so large and so appealing by then that the CBS network bought the Yankees for $11.2 million (NBC's Chet Huntley described the deal as "just one more reason to hate the Yankees"). Mantle and Maris joined the "Tiffany network" lineup of Colonel Klink, Gilligan, Gomer Pyle and a pig named Arnold Ziffel.

Just what CBS had in mind for the team is still unclear, not unlike its decision to green-light *Mayberry RFD*. The network never really tried to make Yankees games part of its programming (CBS relinquished the national baseball contract to NBC two years after the purchase) and made terrible decisions in the baseball front office (firing both Allen and Red Barber). After eight seasons under CBS, the Yankees' TV rights had dropped to $200,000 a year and they were literally paying a station to carry their games on radio. Apparently, the people running the Yankees broadcasting were not the same people who gave us *All in the Family* and *The Mary Tyler Moore Show*.

CBS finally gave up on the Yankees in 1973 and sold the club for less than the 1964 purchase price, having completely blown the opportunity to turn the team into a cable TV bonanza worth $100 million per year. Unfortunately for baseball fans, Steinbrenner did not let that ball roll Buckner-like between his legs.

After first ordering a lifetime supply of pink slips, Steinbrenner directed his efforts at increasing the team's TV revenue, and increase them he did. Spectacularly. By 1987, the Yankees' TV rights had swelled larger than Reggie's ego—to nearly $19 million per season—and that was virtual lunch money compared to the landmark deal Steinbrenner signed with the Madison Square Garden Network the next year. In the biggest media deal that did not include funding for Kevin Costner's *Waterworld*, MSG agreed to give the Yankees $490 million over twelve years. The average annual payments not only were roughly twenty times what teams such as the Twins and Mariners received then for their local rights, the total package was considerably more than the estimated value of the team. For that kind of money, MSG should have been able to install their broadcast booth inside Jeter's bedroom.

Michael Kay: Jeter goes into the stretch . . . Here's his pitch . . . He connects . . . He gets to first base . . . He gets to second base . . . He gets to third base . . . And he scores!!!

John Sterling: Yankees win! Thhhuuuuuhhhhhh Yankees win!!!

Jim Kaat: It's only May, but it looks like Jeter will lead the Yankees in scoring again.

The average annual payments also were roughly double the Yankees' payroll at first, allowing the team to turn a profit before a single ticket was sold. Flush with cash, Steinbrenner kept spending it until he had increased his team's payroll to $114 million in the last year of the contract. It dropped to $110 million the next year, when the Yankees didn't win the World Series for the first time since 1997.

Obviously, Steinbrenner needed to spend more money on the team and the YES Network was just the vehicle.

The YES Network Programming Guide

Programming schedule for Wednesday, September 15

5:15 a.m. *Sunrise Sermonette*—Yankee Stadium announcer Bob Sheppard begins the broadcast day with a message about the glories of the Yankees and Steinbrenner (fifteen minutes).

5:30 a.m. *Yankeecise*—Jason Giambi's personal trainer and Jeter's girlfriends lead an invigorating jazzercise aerobics class (thirty minutes).

6:00 a.m. *161st Street*—Join popular Muppet-hosts Bert and Bernie (ex-Yankee Bert Campaneris and center fielder Bernie Williams) for this educational children's show that teaches kids how to spell the names of Yankees players and count the Yankees championships via meetings with the colorful denizens around Yankee Stadium—Groper, Oscar the Grouchy Homeless Person, Mr. Scalper and Kermit the Heroin Addict (one hour).

7 a.m. The *Today* show—Katie Couric, Matt Lauer and weatherman Don Zimmer host popular morning news and features show. Scheduled guest: former mayor Rudy Giuliani (one hour).

8:00 a.m. *The Bronx Zoo*—Former Yankees reliever Sparky Lyle and Bronx Zoo curator Jim Doherty explore the incredible world of animals. Today: the feeding habits of Giambi and Kevin Brown (one hour).

9:00 a.m. *The Price Is Not Right*—Contestants repeatedly bid too low when asked to guess the price of Yankees tickets (thirty minutes).

9:30 a.m. *This Old House That Ruth Built*—Yankees owner George Steinbrenner explains how Yankee Stadium presents an impossible rebuilding project and why the team needs and deserves a new $1 billion stadium. Special guest: Rudy Giuliani (thirty minutes).

10:00 a.m. *Live with Brosius and Kelly*—Former third baseman Scott Brosius and former Yankees infielder Pat Kelly host popular talk show. Scheduled guests: *61** director Billy Crystal, *Sex and the City* star and Yankees fan Sarah Jessica Parker and world-renowned opera singer Ronan Tynan (one hour).

11:00 a.m. *Style with Elsa Klensch*—YES Network's fashion editor reports from Milan, Paris and the Bronx on the newest hot trend, pinstripes and platinum World Series rings (thirty minutes).

11:30 a.m. *Yankeeography*—Season premiere! The Yanky-winning series returns with the outstanding career of Yankee great Joe Pepitone (one hour).

12:30 p.m. *Days of Our Yankees*—Soap opera. Jason is subpoenaed to appear before a grand jury, Derek is harassed by a stalker, Alex joins a book club (thirty minutes).

1 p.m. *All My Children*—Soap opera based on former Yankees outfielder Luis Polonia's girlfriends (thirty minutes).

1:30 p.m. *Leave It to Zimmer*—The fun begins when Whitey Ford tricks Zimmer into climbing onto the Cup o' Noodles billboard in Times Square—only to have him fall in! After Zimmer is rescued by the fire department, he gets a good talking to from Joe Torre (R) (thirty minutes).

2:00 p.m. *I Love Zimmer*—The fun begins when Zimmer endorses Vitametavegamin during a live commercial, not realizing the health tonic is packed with alcohol! Torre has to leave the club to bring the tipsy Zimmer home (R) (thirty minutes).

2:30 p.m. *Zimmer's Island*—The fun begins after a sudden storm sinks a three-hour Circle Line cruise, stranding Zimmer and the crew on Manhattan island. Skipper Joe Torre nearly gets them off the island, but Zimmer breaks the transmitter and gives the cab driver bad directions! (R) (thirty minutes).

3:00 p.m. *TRL*—Host Carson Daly welcomes the day's hottest musical acts. Scheduled guests: Liza Minnelli sings "New York, New York" and Mariah Carey sings "Happy Birthday" to Jeter (one hour).

4:00 p.m. *Trading Players*—Neighboring teams remodel each other's roster over a weekend without going over a budget of $200 million. Today, Texas designer Tom Hicks gives A-Rod to the Yankees, while Brian Cashman gives Hicks second baseman Alfonso Soriano and a color scheme to be named later (one hour).

5:00 p.m. *The O'Neill-Leyritz Report*—Former Yankees right fielder Paul O'Neill and former catcher Jim Leyritz deliver a thoughtful recount of how the day's major national and international news affects the Yankees pennant chances, along with an analysis of terrible umpires (thirty minutes).

5:30 p.m. *Who Wants to Be a Multimillionaire?*—Cashman negotiates with agents over $140 million, eight-year Yankees contracts for their clients (thirty minutes).

6:00 p.m. *South Parking Lot*—Surly, crude, foulmouthed attendants charge a small fortune to park cars in the Yankee Stadium ramp (thirty minutes).

6:30 p.m. *Yankees History Channel*—A look at how the Yankees compare to other great empires (see page 164 for more details, thirty minutes).

7:00 p.m. Yankees vs. Red Sox. (Not available in most markets. Instead YES will rerun the *Seinfeld* episode where George takes a job as the Yankees assistant traveling secretary: thirty minutes).

7:30 p.m. *Survivor*—Reality show pits contestants against each other in a life-and-death struggle to see who can wear a Red Sox cap the longest in the Yankee Stadium bleachers (thirty minutes).

8:00 p.m. *Sex and the City*—Documentary following forty-eight hours in the life of Jeter (thirty minutes).

8:30 p.m. *The Apprentice*—Reality show pits contestants against each other in bitter boardroom fights for the grand prize—a one-year contract working for Steinbrenner. Second prize is a two-year contract (thirty minutes).

9:00 p.m. *The Sopranos*—Drama about the many girlfriends of world-renowned opera tenor Ronan Tynan (thirty minutes).

9:30 p.m. *ER*—Doctors perform emergency brain surgery on catcher Mike Piazza after another confrontation with Clemens. Giambi gets scoped. Zimmer goes in for a replacement steel plate (thirty minutes).

10:00 p.m. *That '70s Show*—Reggie and Billy fight in the dugout over a girl they both like (thirty minutes).

10:30 p.m. *NYPD Blue*—Detectives Sipowicz and Sorenson bust a dangerous ring of crooks selling unlicensed Yankees merchandise. Detectives Medavoy and Jones earn extra money moonlighting as security guards at Yankee Stadium. Detective McDowell receives a tip from informant Howie Spira (thirty minutes).

11:00 p.m. *11 O'clock News*—Roundup of all the day's news concerning the Yankees, much of it involving Darryl Strawberry (thirty minutes).

11:30 p.m. *The Tonight Show with Michael Kay*—Kay's scheduled guests: *Sex and the City* star Sarah Jessica Parker talks about her secret love affair with the Yankees; mimes Steve Shields and Ed Yarnall perform their celebrated "Giambi Running from First to Third Against the Wind" routine. Band director: Eddie Layton (ninety minutes).

1:00 a.m. The Late Movie, *Pride of the Yankees*—Gary Cooper stars as Yankees great Lou Gehrig in nightly showing of the greatest movie ever made (letterbox, two hours).

3:00 a.m. *The 700 Club*—Religious show based on devotion to Yankees who have driven in more than 700 runs (one hour).

4:00 a.m. *Incredible Inventions*—Host Ron Popeil offers an incredible range of new products, including the David Wells's six-pack abs rowing machine, Joe Pepitone's instant hair and the Oscar Gamble Chia Pet (one hour).

5:00 a.m. *Sign-Off*—Bob Merrill sings the national anthem, followed by Ronan Tynan singing "God Bless America" and the Mormon Tabernacle Choir singing "Cotton Eye Joe."

Creating Yank-Jazeera provided Steinbrenner such hefty amounts of cash that he has to hire extra interns to carry him around in the sedan chair when he receives the monthly payments. Sports business analyst Andrew Zimbalist estimated in his book *May the Best Team Win* that the YES Network generated as much as $160 million in revenue its first year, while *Forbes* estimated it would bring in $200 million in 2003. The best guess is that the Yankees will make $150 million in annual profit from YES within a few years. And thanks to accounting schemes so complicated, they would baffle Enron executives, they won't have to apply all of it toward revenue sharing (Atlanta and the Red Sox have similar deals).

The channel started in controversy—when Yank-Jazeera debuted in 2002, the Yankees were still bickering over fees with Cablevision, with the delicious result that broadcasts of the first games of that season were not available in major sections of the city (fans only learned the scores through an elaborate system of smoke signals, semaphores, carrier pigeons and Morse Code), and then the situation grew much, much worse. The two sides signed a truce, ending Yankee Free

Manhattan and providing New York fans the long-sought opportunity to watch documentaries on Moose Skowron and replays of New York games that had originally been played forty years earlier.

Thanks to the YES Network and satellite TV, the Yankees are now as ubiquitous in this country as poker tournaments and Andy Griffith reruns. If fans thought they could at least escape Yankees broadcasts by fleeing the country, Steinbrenner stymied them again by signing a deal with the Yomiuri Giants in 2002 that led to virtually all of New York's games being shown in Japan as well, allowing citizens of that country to enjoy the same stimulating entertainment and thoughtful dialogue so thoroughly enjoyed by millions of Americans.

"Konnichiwa, minasan. America no hokori wo, tano kuni no hito-bito to wakachi aukoto ga dekite, kouei desu. Yankee stadium no so-togawa no sekai ga kuzureyouto shiteirutoki, wareware wa mada, subarashii otokotati ga sikkari to wareware wo daihyousite kure-teiru—sou omoeru koto de, gennki zuke rare masu. Sah, soredewa, suponsa no kotoba to tomoni, Derek Jeter san wo, shoukai shimasyo."

"Arigatou gozaimasu, Steiner-san. Kodomo tachi wa minnna wak-katteru to omoukedo, ookina shiai nomaetteiuno wa, tottemo kincho surukara, Chesterfield no mensol no kaori wo kaguto, kimochi ga ochitsukunda."

Not satisfied with the official MLB-run Yankees.com Internet site, New York has YESNetwork.com, where users can link to regular columns espousing the team's glories, such as "Kitty Kaboodle" by Jim Kaat, "Charley's Chatter" by Charley Steiner and "Pep Talk" by Phil Pepe (but alas, no "Giuliani's Jewels" by the ex-mayor).

Now that the Yankees have conquered cable television, radio and the Internet, what does the future hold? It's difficult to imagine that New York could expand its media empire further, but at one point it also was difficult to imagine that Regis Philbin would have a workout video. Undoubtedly, NASA engineers and Yankees interns are already hard at work on a new matrix that will allow fans to pipe into a fabulous array of new content. As soon as they work out a few bugs, YES Matrix representatives will personally offer fans the option of the Blue Package or the Red Package. If fans choose the Blue Package, they will forget about the YES Matrix offer and return to their regular YES Network package of games and *Yankeeography* documentaries. But if they choose the Red Package, they will be hooked into the YES Matrix and receive on-demand clubhouse access, original dramas, comedies and concerts, live broadcasts of games, director's-cut replays of games with optional endings, broadcasts of games from 1927 that were never filmed, broadcasts of games from 2034 that haven't been played yet and a spectacular virtual reality Pay-Per-View that will allow fans to actually play in the games they are watching without ever leaving their couches or setting down their beers.

The beauty of it for Steinbrenner is that no matter which package the fans choose, he'll bill them the same $79.95 monthly charge.

Until that day comes, however, just be thankful that there isn't YES-SPAN and YES-SPAN 2.

Of course, the way the damn Yankees work, those are probably just a matter of time.

The YES Network Presents the Yankees History Channel

Voice-over: "The Yankees History Channel presents 'World Empires' with your host, Hizzonor Rudy Giuliani."

Giuliani: "Good evening.

"Born in 1903, the Yankees Empire rose to world power with the purchase of Babe Ruth in 1919. Eighty-six years and twenty-six world championships later, the empire is stronger than ever, the richest and most successful sports dynasty in history.

"Under the magnificent rule of owner George Steinbrenner III, the Yankees have won regular-season games on two continents, three countries, five time zones, seventeen states and twenty-four counties, plus the District of Columbia. The Yankees have employed players from more than twenty nations and established marketing partners in Europe and Japan. Their logo is as recognized worldwide—and dare I say respected?—as the Stars and Stripes. They have brought joy to countless millions of fans around the globe.

"Baseball fans already know the vast superiority the Yankees hold over the Red Sox, the Mets and all the other major league teams. But how do the Yankees stack up against the Roman Empire? How do the 1949 to 1964 Yankees match up with the best of the British Empire? Would the Mongols be able to handle the pressure of October in Yankee Stadium?

"And most importantly, who would win a seven-game series between the 1998 Yankees and the 1962 Soviets?

"Tonight on the Yankees History Channel, we gather a panel of historians to compare the Yankees to the other great empires in world history. Our first guest is Sir Anthony Rhodes, the world-renowned professor of archaeology at the University of Cairo, to discuss the Egyptians."

Rhodes: "The pharaohs ruled Egypt for more than two thousand years, taming and cultivating the desert four millennia before air conditioning. The Egyptians left behind the awe-inspiring pyramids and their spectacularly preserved mummies of King Tutankhamen and Ramses II as evidence of their highly advanced culture."

Giuliani: "Very interesting, but you want awe-inspiring pyramids? You should see the piles of ticker tape Yankees fans leave after each World Series championship—the overtime from the city sanitation crews almost put us in the red every year. And you haven't seen a spectacularly preserved mummy until you've seen Zimmer as our bench coach. Edge to the Yankees.

"Next up, we have to get right to Dr. Constantine Pappas, dean of history at the University of Athens, the world's leading authority on Bronze Age Greece."

Pappas: "Considered the cradle of Western civilization, ancient Greece touched most of the known world under Alexander the Great before falling to the Romans in 146 BC. Nonetheless, Greece's legacy lives on in virtually every aspect of our lives—philosophy, medicine, democracy, drama, mathematics, geometry, architecture and sport. More than two millennia after Greece's fall, we still have the Parthenon, the Hippocratic Oath, Homer's *Odyssey*."

Giuliani: "And let's not forget the Olympics, which should go to the greatest city in the world in 2012—no other city deserves it more than the Big Apple, New York City. The Greek legacy is certainly impressive, but so is New York's—the Yankees gave us the Ballantine Blast, the Bronx Cheer and David Wells's memoir, *Perfect I'm Not*.

Pappas: "Seriously, sir. I would have to give the edge to the Greeks."

Giuliani: "Maybe, but not by much.

"Next, we have Professor Alexander DeLaurenti, professor emeritus at Columbia University, who will tell us about the Romans."

DeLaurenti: "At its full glory, Rome controlled most of Europe and the Mediterranean, ruling for more than five hundred years before collapsing in the fourth century under the attack of the Vandals and Visigoths. If I may interject a bit of humor here, as Monty Python points out so wonderfully in *Life of Brian,* 'Apart from the sanitation, the medicine, education, wine, public order, irrigation, roads, a fresh-water system and public health, what have the Romans ever done for us?' "

Giuliani: "Weren't there also those marvelous spectacles in the Coliseum, where up to fifty thousand spectators would watch the Romans feed Christians to the lions, force gladiators to fight to their deaths and pit desperate men against hungry animals?"

DeLaurenti: "Yes, it is one of Rome's lesser contributions."

Giuliani: "Well, Steinbrenner regularly feeds the Tigers to the Yankees at Yankee Stadium, though I have to admit, he has yet to lick the sanitation, fresh-water and road dilemma. The wine problem has pretty much been solved. Let's call it a draw. But that will undoubtedly change when the Yankees get the new stadium they so clearly need.

"Next, Professor Chang Eng of the University of Singapore to discuss the Mongol Empire.

Eng: "At one point reaching from Beijing to present-day Hungary, the Mongol Empire may have been history's largest in overall territory. The infamous Genghis Kahn created the empire and gathered his territory through brilliant military strategy, an intimidating, superbly trained cavalry and ruthless tactics—towns that did not surrender to him were literally destroyed. The Mongol Empire was relatively short-lived, however, lasting barely a century after it took control of Beijing."

Giuliani: "Sure, Doc, the Mongols had their way with remote, defenseless villages in outer Mongolia, but I doubt they would have had such an easy time with the Bronx—your precious Genghis Khan wouldn't have gotten off the subway platform. And you want to see warriors on horseback—try running onto the field when New York's finest has its horse patrol on duty at the end of a clinching game in the postseason. Believe me, nobody gets by my guys. Besides, Steinbrenner sent the Yankees into Asia in 2004 and regularly pillages the city of Boston whenever it gets in his way."

Eng: "So you're giving the edge to a baseball team?"

Giuliani: "No, not *just* a baseball team—the New York Yankees. Next, Dr. Toby Atwood, dean of history at Trinity College, Dublin, on the British Empire."

Atwood: "At the height of its power in the early twentieth century, the British controlled one-fourth of the earth's land mass and one-fourth of its population, with territory on every continent. It was said that the sun never set on the British Empire during its peak, but it finally slipped below the horizon following World War Two, most notably when India gained its independence in 1947."

Giuliani: "Yankee ingenuity solved that sundown problem on this side of the pond. New York wisely installed lights at Yankee Stadium in 1946, allowing the team to play night games and increase its revenue, then reached the World Series in ten of the next twelve seasons."

Atwood: "Let me guess. Edge to the Yankees?"

Giuliani: "And to His Majesty, King George III.

"Finally, we come to the specific question: Who would win a seven-game series between the 1998 Yankees and the 1962 Soviet Empire? To answer that, we asked award-winning YES broadcaster John Sterling to handicap both empires."

Sterling: "The Soviets are a worthy opponent, no doubt about it. They had the hydrogen bomb, held territory from the Kamchatka peninsula to the Alps, commanded one of the world's largest and best-trained armies and had just built the Berlin Wall and begun installing tactical nuclear weapons in Cuba, putting the entire eastern seaboard into missile range. They loomed as a greater threat to the free world than at any other point in their history.

"But remember that the Yankees won 114 games during the regular season that year, plus eleven more in the postseason, including a four-game sweep of the Padres in the World Series. They had a dependable starting rotation, a deep bullpen and a lineup that was solid one to nine. The depth of the Soviet Union's alcoholism is well documented but the Yankees had no such trouble—even half drunk, David Wells was able to pitch a perfect game. And frankly, how could Nikita Khrushchev possibly match the leadership provided by the incomparable Paulie O'Neill?

"Sure, the Soviets might be able to win a game or two, but no way would that series go more than six games before New York clinches it with Mariano Rivera closing it out in the ninth. *Yankees win! Thhhuuuuuuuhhhhhh Yankees win!*"

Giuliani: "Thank you, John.

"And now that we've established the superiority of the Yankees Empire, the more important question is whether the Yankees can overcome the internal and external forces that destroyed the great empires that came before them. Could the Yankees possibly go the way of the Mongols, the Egyptians and the Soviets? It's a considerable challenge for Torre and Cashman, even with both A-Rod and Jeets in the same infield, but it won't happen as long as the great Steinbrenner rules.

"Everyone, however, must do their part to protect the realm. The lesson of history is that empires begin dying as soon as they cease expanding, which is why the Yankees need a new stadium. Call the mayor today and insist that he make the stadium a reality so that the Yankees Empire grows even stronger in its second century.

"For the Yankee History Channel, I'm Rudy Giuliani. Good night."

Voice-over: "Coming up on the Yankee History Channel, we look at Yankee Stadium's 138-foot-high baseball bat/exhaust tower on *Modern Yankee Marvels*."

CHAPTER 10

The Fourth Estate

The world used more than 300 million tons of paper in 2003. Of that staggering total, 8 percent was accounted for by copies of *The Da Vinci Code,* 13 percent by copies of the NCAA rule book, 15 percent by NCAA tournament brackets in office pools, 19 percent by preapproved credit card offers sent through the mail and the remaining percent by newspaper and magazine stories about Derek Jeter.

Am I exaggerating? Perhaps, but not much. So much is written about the Yankees that if Jeter ever dated J-Lo, Weyerhaeuser wouldn't be able to cut down enough trees to satisfy newsprint demands. The Yankees not only win more games than everyone else, they swallow up so much media coverage that *Entertainment Tonight* is down to just two correspondents on Paris Hilton.

This isn't a massive conspiracy engineered by the liberal media (relax and count to ten, Ann) or the Bush administration neocons (put the camera down, Michael). To paraphrase former House Speaker Tip O'Neill, all sports is local. Most of the major magazine and book publishers are located in New York, and naturally their editors are most interested in the New York teams (as are their bookies). There are also so many people rooting for and against New York teams nationwide that publishers know they can always sell enough copies to make publication worthwhile, which isn't the case with, say, the Tampa Bay Devil Rays. It's simple supply and demand.

Of course, none of this makes it any easier for the rest of us to see Jeter and his fellow Yankees on more magazine covers than Princess Di ever was.

The Yankees have been on the cover of *Sports Illustrated* more than any other sports team, which is reasonable given their many championships over the past half century. But is there any reason that Steinbrenner has been on the cover more times (four) than Rickey Henderson (three times, and one of those was when Rickey played for the Yankees)? Or that from 1990 to 2003 Rickey would win the MVP award, break the career stolen base record, break the career walk record, break the career runs record and play in the postseason six years, yet still be on *SI*'s cover less often during that span than Mantle (last game, 1968), DiMaggio (last game, 1950) or Ruth (last game, 1935) each was?

It simply doesn't pay to play farther from the New York market than a reporter will be reimbursed on his expense sheets.

Barry Bonds, the greatest player of his generation and inarguably among the ten greatest in baseball history, has played his entire career in San Francisco and Pittsburgh. At last glance, he had been the cover subject for *Sports Illustrated* four times, the same number as Elle McPherson. Jeter has been on the cover eight times, including one time after he was batting .189.

As the country's largest city, New York has more daily newspapers than anywhere else. The *Times*, the *Post* and the *Daily News* in the city, plus *Newsday*, the Newark *Star-Ledger*, the *Bergen Record*, the *Journal News* and the *Hartford Courant* all have beat reporters covering and traveling with the Yankees on a daily basis. And then there are the dozens of Japanese reporters shadowing Hideki Matsui so religiously that one paper hired a helicopter to photograph him running in the Yankee Stadium outfield for the first time, networks broadcast his first batting practice live in Japan and one paper ran a photo of his mouth on page one when he had a root canal. There were so many Japanese reporters covering Matsui that, at one point, the Yankees literally limited their numbers in the clubhouse.

"Sorry, sir, only three at a time."

"You do not understand. I must get inside. My editor will fire me if I don't find out whether Matsui-san is wearing boxers or briefs today."

With so many sports reporters assigned full-time to the Yankees, it's a wonder we were able to get any details about Kobe Bryant's pending trial.

No other team has so many writers adding so many words so regularly to its franchise mythology. There are even more writers extolling the virtues of the Yankees than there were whining about the fate of the Red Sox.

"Beginning in the 1920s, New York City had probably the greatest collection of sportswriters ever," says Glenn Stout, author of *Yankees Century* and a leading authority on the history of sportswriting. "They had Damon Runyan, Heywood Broun, John Kieran, Dan Daniel. . . . That you had the best writers in one city and that you had Babe Ruth playing there, that necessarily made the Yankees stand out even a little more than they should have. You had all those writers competing and trying to outdo each other.

"New York was the largest city, and the media capital of the country, and I think the writers knew they were writing for posterity."

These New York writers from a very different age in journalism turned Ruth into a legend—embellishing the facts so much when writing about the Called Shot and little Johnny Sylvester that they should have had their creative licenses revoked—while hiding his less-admirable traits (public drunkenness, rampant whoring). The same was true with coverage of DiMaggio and Mantle.

"Some of the writing gets pretty purple, but at the same time it was very memorable," Stout says. "Ruth is a great example of how much that stuff stuck. Almost all we know about Ruth is in the phrases of the writers who covered him. The House That Ruth Built, the Sultan of Swat.

"Back then, by and large, they saw themselves as members of the organization. Their job was to tout the players, and with the Yankees winning all the time, it was easy to tout them. DiMaggio is a great example. He gave them nothing. He was a blank slate and they filled in the personality on top of it. Jeter, in a way, is following the same mold. He talks but says nothing. So in the end, all you can write about is how they play."

Sports journalism has changed considerably since then, and later generations haven't been the slightest bit shy about revealing the shadier side of the Yankees' personalities—writing up Billy's misadventures was such a part of daily coverage that there should have been a line in the boxscore: *Heinekens, Martin 2*. Nonetheless, modern writers too have steadily built up the Yankee story. The great Steinbrenner-Billy-Reggie saga made for tremendous copy, as has the recent intensity of the Yankees–Red Sox rivalry. Whether they have reported positive stories about the Yankees or negative stories about the Yankees, in the end the important thing is they have reported about the Yankees.

Whatever the Yankees do, there's going to be a story about it. As Yankees PR director Rick Cerrone told *Sports Illustrated*'s Charles Pierce, "We're always at DefCon Four. It doesn't take much to get us to DefCon Five."

"There is always something happening," says *Newsday* columnist Jon Heyman, who has covered and written about the Yankees for fifteen years. "Someone is always getting yelled at, someone is always getting acquired, somebody is always getting fired. There are teams like in Milwaukee or in Montreal that may make two big deals every year. In New York, there's news every day.

"The GMs are nervous fellows. They either eat a lot and get very fat or they eat very little and get very skinny. Brian Cashman only eats Tums and for a while one season, he was down to about ninety-eight pounds. It's a nervous job and they know that when they talk to us there's always the potential to get in trouble if they say the wrong thing."

Covering the Yankees is a relentless, demanding, draining job. The competition is so keen for news and Steinbrenner so volatile that in addition to their beat writers, papers assign reporters to stalk the owner so closely you would think he was running for office (heaven forbid).

"Normally, there are younger, less experienced guys assigned to that duty. Because it yields next to nothing," Heyman says. "You just trail him around for hours hoping that he'll grunt or do something, but in recent years he's said nothing or just uttered some trite sayings that he must have dug up from *Bartlett's*.

"They stand outside his suite and then they follow him to the car, which is sometimes waiting right at the entrance. And he walks pretty briskly for a guy in his seventies so he doesn't give them much chance to ask questions. We're all wasting our time on the off chance he'll say something. Even if he says something mildly negative it's news."

(The worst part of the job, however, may be working in the suffocating pressroom, located in the bowels of Yankee Stadium. There are no windows, not enough phones, not enough desk space and the air is so stale you can still smell the lingering odor from Dick Young's famous Independence Day Fart of 1963.)

The rise of sports talk radio and the Internet only adds to the crushing coverage. The Yankees are the topic of so many radio talk shows nationwide that I'm surprised Rush Limbaugh doesn't weigh in regularly. *The Yankees never would have lost the World Series after 9/11 had it not been for Bill Clinton*. But this, too, makes sense. If you have to fill twenty-four hours of airtime each day, and if you're going to syndicate radio shows nationwide, talking about those damn Pittsburgh Pirates all the time won't do much for your afternoon drive-time ratings.

"Take the ESPN radio network," Stout says. "If you're going to be a national network, you have to talk about the team that's the most famous and popular in the country. There have been surveys that show fifteen percent of baseball fans identify themselves as fans of the Yankees. You put the Yankees and the Red Sox together, and you have about a quarter of the country either loving them or hating them."

And, either way, interested enough in them to turn every bit of Yankees news into a subject of raging argument, driving debate across the country.

"John from Teaneck, you're on Mike and the Mad Dog.*"*

"Yeah, I just want to ask whether you know whether Matsui was given an injection of Novocain when he got the root canal or whether they gave him nitrous oxide."

"I think it was Novocain, John."

"What the hell were those idiots thinking?"

The New York Times *Worst-Seller List*

A recent search for "New York Yankees" on Amazon.com turned up more than two hundred books about the team—and those are just the books that haven't been out of print so long that the company can't find a used edition underneath a beer stool somewhere.

Of course, there are some Yankees books you may have trouble ordering:

1. *Tuesday with Maury* by Mitch Albom   The bestselling writer reveals the valuable lessons former Dodgers infielder Maury Wills taught his Los Angeles teammates on the workout day before they swept the Yankees in the 1963 World Series.

2. *Pull My Finger: The Collected Verse of Thurman Munson* Found poetry pulled from Munson's everyday clubhouse conversation, including his classic haiku, "Interview at the Postgame Spread":

> *Are you deaf or what?*
> *I said @$%# off! no comment;*
> *Pass the damn steak (belch)*

3. *Who Hit My Cheese?* by Spencer Johnson and Kevin Brown The pitcher's diary of pitching for the Yankees, with tips on interior wall repair.

4. *You're Fired! Management Lessons from the Bronx Bombers* by George Steinbrenner   The Yankees owner explains his business secrets.

5. *Moneybags* by Michael Lewis   In a follow-up to his 2003 best-seller, the *Wall Street Journal* reporter explains how general manager Brian Cashman is able to compete year after year with the highest payroll in baseball.

6. *@$%# You! The Wit and Wisdom of Billy Martin* edited by Maury Allen   A collection of the late manager's greatest quotes, including "What the hell are you looking at?" and "You better shut the @$%# up before I kick your ass" and "Can I apply the cover charge to a lap dance?"

7. *Balfour* by Jim Bouton   The former pitcher's tell-all, behind-the-door look at the jewelry company that produces the Yankees' world championship rings.

8. *The DiMaggio Code* by Dan Brown   Thriller follows cryptologist and his beautiful assistant as they attempt to unravel ancient mystery surrounding what items the famed Yankee Clipper would sign at autograph shows.

9. *Paper or Plastic? I'll Take Plastic, I Guess, It's Easier to Carry* by Yogi Berra   A collection of Yogi quotes that weren't particularly funny, convoluted or memorable, including "That pitch looked a little outside, Ump" and "I'm going to pinch-hit for Kemp" and "Super-size me, please."

10. *George Steinbrenner Is a Big Fat Idiot* by Al Franken   Blistering mix of fact and satire on the infamous Yankees owner.

Shhh, No Jeering in the Library

Unfortunately, not even our libraries are safe.

James Thurber wrote "The majority of American males put themselves to sleep by striking out the batting order of the New York Yankees." Philip Roth complains in *The Great American Novel* that Yogi wasn't voted into the Hall of Fame in his first year of eligibility.

Faulkner refers to Ruth and the Yankees in *The Sound and the Fury*. And Hemingway has the old fisherman in *The Old Man and the Sea* say, "I would like to take the great DiMaggio fishing" and "I think the great DiMaggio would be proud of me today."

It was Yogi, though, who when told Hemingway was a great writer, replied, "Yeah, for what paper?"

Yogi, naturally, has done his own part in weighing down the nation's bookshelves, with four books that use one of his famous quotes in the title—*Yogi: It Ain't Over; When You Come to a Fork in the Road, Take It; What Time Is It? You Mean Now?* and *I Really Didn't Say Everything I Said*. Of course, that's nothing compared to Mantle, who has at least two dozen biographies devoted to him, including three by the Mick and a ghostwriter. (Before he died, I think he was working on *My Least Favorite January*, an account of the year Mantle spent a couple weeks in January snowed in at his in-laws.)

There are so many Yankees books that they've run out of titles.

There is *The Year the Yankees Lost the Pennant*, the novel by Douglass Wallop that was the basis for the musical *Damn Yankees*: *The Billy Martin Story* by Maury Allen; *Damned Yankees*, the terrific behind-the-scenes book by Bill Madden and Moss Klein; and *Those Damn Yankees: The Secret Life of America's Greatest Franchise* by Dean Chadwin.

There is *Where Have All Our Yankees Gone?* by Brian Jensen and *Yankees: Where Have You Gone?* by Maury Allen.

Are the Yankees coming or going? There is Robert Creamer's classic *Babe: The Legend Comes to Life* and Jim Reisler's recent *Babe Ruth: Launching the Legend*. And there also is *Last Hero*, David Falkner's biography of Mickey Mantle; *The Last Yankee*, Falkner's biography of Billy Martin; and *The Last Night of the Yankee Dynasty*, Buster Olney's terrific recap of the most recent New York teams.

The Yankees are so proud their chroniclers can't decide who they're proud of most. There is *Lou Gehrig, Pride of the Yankees* by Paul Gallico, *Derek Jeter: Pride of the Yankees* by Patrick Giles, and *Pride of October* by Bill Madden (about all the Yankees).

So many Yankees books have October in the title that the team must own the copyright on the month. In addition to Madden's book, there is Roger Kahn's *October Men*, David Halberstam's *October 1964*, Maury Allen's *Mr. October*, Sal Maiorana's *A Lifetime of Yankee Octobers* and, of course, Mantle's *All My Octobers*.

Not content with one mere month, there are books dedicated to select years (John Mosedale's *The Greatest of All* on the 1927 team, Rich Tofel's *A Legend in the Making* on the 1939 season, Halberstam's *Summer of '49*, Mantle's *My Favorite Summer: 1956*, Tony Kubek's *Sixty-One*, and *Champions!*, about the 1996 season, by Bob Klapisch and John Harper).

You can follow the Yankees history through a series of books, beginning with *Before They Were Bombers*, Jim Reisler's history of the team from 1903 to 1915; *Dynasty*, Peter Golenbock's history from 1949 to 1964; *Dog Days*, Philip Bashe's history from 1964 to 1976; and the ubiquitous Maury Allen's *All Roads Lead to October*, which covers the Steinbrenner years up to 1999.

In fact, the Yankees have appropriated the entire twentieth century. There is Stout's excellent *Yankees Century*, Harry Frommer's *A Yankees Century*, Alan Ross's *The Yankees Century*, and The Sporting News's *The Yankees: A Century of Greatness*.

Think there is a slice of the Yankees uncovered? Guess again. There are at least five books just about Yankee Stadium. There is a collection of legal essays on the Yankees (*Courting the Yankees* by Ettie Ward). There is a book by Paul O'Neill about his father (*Me and My Dad*). There is a self-help book by Darryl Strawberry (*Recovering Life*).

When picking up prostitutes, make sure they aren't undercover cops. Especially when you're on probation.

There is even a business leadership book based on lessons learned from Billy Martin's style (*Dugout Days* by Michael DeMarco).

Lesson one: Don't drink on the job.

Lesson two: Don't call your boss a convicted liar. At least not in the newspaper.

Lesson three: Don't beat up your employees.

There is *The Wit and Wisdom of Yogi Berra*, which is not to be confused with *The Zen of Zim* or *O Holy Cow!: The Selected Verse of Phil Rizzuto*, all of which are real books (though I'm not sure whether the Rizzuto collection includes the Scooter's 1978 bulletin that the Pope had just died: "Well, that kind of puts a damper on even a Yankees win").

Even David Wells hit the bestseller list with *Perfect I'm Not*, no doubt giving him the rare distinction of writing a book before he read one.

With so many Yankees fans around the country and in the publishing world, the question is not how Zimmer, Yogi and Boomer could all have had books on the *New York Times* bestseller list; the question is how come we have yet to see a *South Bronx Diet* book soar to the top of the list.

So now, here I am with yet another book on the Yankees. On the one hand, at least I'm offering some desperately needed balance to the Yankees propaganda. On the other hand, I know—I just know—that my book will end up getting buried between copies of *Zim: A Baseball Life* and *The Zen of Zim*.

Grrrrrr. . . .

 ### *The South Bronx Diet*

"Down in front, fatso! You're blocking the right side of the infield.

"Yeah, I'm talking to you, Lard-Ass. Boy, it looks like the Atkins plan is really working wonders for you. That's the worst-looking figure I've seen in Yankee Stadium since they flashed Jeff Weaver's ERA on the scoreboard. And did anyone tell you that when you buy a team replica jersey it's not supposed to fit the entire team? Cripes, with that many X's and L's, your size tag looks like the Super Bowl logo. Where did you buy that anyway, the Big,

Fat and Disgusting Store or did Ringling Bros. just hold their annual tent sale?

"Seeing as you got season tickets and given that I would like to see the second baseman sometime before October, I've got a little diet tip. Forget that Atkins crap and get on the South Bronx Diet. The beauty of this diet is there are no carb restrictions, no calorie counting, no food zones, no fat limits, no point system and no dieting. That's right. You can eat anything you want and as much as you want, which I think is a plan that even a Michelin Man like you can follow.

"Sounds too good to be true, doesn't it, Tubby? Yeah, well, so did the A-Rod trade, but it was. True, there is one small catch to the South Bronx Diet. You have to buy all your food at the Yankee Stadium concession stands and at concession prices. Sure, that crap is high in calories but you would be amazed at how little of it even a whale like you can actually eat when you have to stand in line for two innings to buy a dog and a beer that cost so much that not even all the players could afford a full meal. You'll lose two pounds just waiting through 'God Bless America.' Plus, the weight practically melts off your body from November to March.

"Sure, that's a long time to go between meals but at least the South Bronx Diet lets you eat in October. It could be worse. You could go on the Tampa Bay Grapefruit Diet."

CHAPTER 11

Solving the Yankees

And so we come to the heart of the matter. Now that the latest New York dynasty has lasted longer than a PBS pledge drive, is there anything that can be done about the Yankees or are they an unstoppable and uncontrollable force, like Starbucks? After all, we can't count on an unprecedented, historic choke every fall.

Realistic solutions exist to the Yankees problem, but we have to be very careful about employing them indiscriminately. On the one hand, we want to disarm the Yankees of their WMD capability so that they no longer pose a constant, overwhelming threat to the American League and humanity in general. On the other hand, we don't want to cripple them like Kathy Bates taking the sledgehammer to James Caan in *Misery* and leave them a helpless victim unable to ever challenge for another championship. After all, we already have the Pirates for that.

Plus, can you imagine how insufferable Red Sox fans would soon become if they now start winning championships on a regular basis?

George Lucas knew that if he was to keep the *Star Wars* franchise alive for three decades, six movies and countless Boba Fett action figures he had to keep Darth Vader and the Galactic Empire around. He realized the key wasn't in eradicating the Empire but in allowing the good guys to win every once in a while. That's all we're looking to do here. We're not looking to kill the Yankees, just blow up their Death Star so some other teams can reach the World Series before they rebuild it. And we need to find a way to do it without using Jar Jar Binks.

We need to harness the Yankees so they remain good enough that beating them and rooting against them and watching them choke a 3–0 lead is still meaningful, but no longer so powerful that our victories are few and far between, that we grow too old to throw an empty beer bottle far enough to reach the field, let alone a player. What we want is something similar to NASCAR placing restrictor plates on cars at Daytona and Talladega. Drivers are prevented from driving at dangerous speeds but they aren't slowed down so much that they get passed by a soccer mom ferrying the neighborhood kids to practice in a minivan.

What can we do about the Yankees? Here are a few possibilities.

1. Three Isn't a Crowd

Roughly 21 million people live in the New York metropolitan market, most of whom will be attempting to use the Major Deegan Expressway the same time you're in a rush to get to work in the morning.

As detailed in other chapters, this fan base gives the Yankees a tremendous competitive advantage over every team in their league. Even if you account for the Mets and their unfortunate fans, the Yankees can still draw from nearly 11 million people while the Pirates, Royals and Brewers combined have barely half that number. Those teams take in so little money that Sally Struthers should be doing commercials for them.

Just $300,000 a month—only one million pennies a day—can bring an effective middle reliever to the impoverished town of Kansas City. . . .

While baseball can't do very much about the populations of small-market cities, it could increase the competition for fans in New York by placing a third team in the area. There were three teams in New York for nearly six decades, after all, and each enjoyed some of their most successful seasons during that period. True, the Dodgers and the Giants both moved, due in part to changing demographics and a (brief) period of falling attendance, but a lot has changed in the past fifty years. This is the twenty-first century, and if New York is large enough to support the egos of Steinbrenner, Giuliani *and* Trump, it's certainly large enough to support three baseball teams.

Adding a third team would have the quickest and most positive effect on the game outside of eliminating organ music. It would dilute the Yankees' broadcasting revenue, and while it would not entirely level the playing field, it would at least guarantee the playing field is no longer as off-kilter as the deck of the *Titanic* an hour after the ship struck the movie's gross revenue.

"Over time you would have parity," Yankees historian Glenn Stout says. "Until that happens the Yankees will continue to suck up all the oxygen and rake in all the money. It's inevitable."

If New York fans had a third team to cheer and if Grey Goose vodka could reach its target audience through another baseball team, the YES Network's revenue streams would narrow enough that Steinbrenner might have to order Cashman out to the parking lot to hold a car wash before signing anyone to a five-year, $120 million contract.

Where to put a team? New Jersey, already home to the Jets, Giants and Nets could serve as a possible home. After all, there is a sufficient population base (the six Jersey counties nearest to New York City have a population of more than 4 million) and sufficient money (the state's household income is roughly 25 percent higher than the U.S. average). The Yankees found it a credible enough area that they hinted about moving there when they were negotiating for a remodeled Yankee Stadium.

On the other hand, it's New Jersey.

A more intriguing location is Brooklyn, the famed New York borough that writers and poets so often nostalgically link with a more innocent era of baseball, when the players were as much a part of the community as striking dockworkers and politicians on the take. The borough never regained its sense of identity and community after it was betrayed that infamous day in the 1950s when Julius and Ethel Rosenberg moved the Dodgers to Los Angeles. (Wait a minute. I got slightly mixed up there. The Rosenbergs didn't move the Dodgers out of Brooklyn; Walter O'Malley did that shortly after he passed along atomic secrets to the Soviets.)

The NBA's New Jersey Nets have already talked about moving to Brooklyn. If major league baseball returned to Brooklyn it would create excitement on a par even greater than if the city repaired the potholes.

Picture Brooklyn native Spike Lee sitting behind the dugout, and heckling Indianapolis Pacers guard Reggie Miller. Imagine a rebuilt Ebbets Field identical to the original with the exceptions of such modern updates as luxury suites, a plasma video replay board and an update to the old Abe Stark sign that reads "Hit Sign, Win Lawsuit." Envision a new "Boys of Summer" roster of players endearing themselves to Brooklyn fans for months and months until the modern equivalents of Gil Hodges and Carl Furillo reach salary arbitration for the first time.

Just as importantly, placing a new team in Brooklyn also would have the side benefit of eliminating the market for further nostalgic stories and books pining about the golden days of the Dodgers. (I mean, really. With our national parklands already opened to logging and the Brazilian rain forests shrinking at the rate of 93,000 acres per day, can we honestly afford to have any more paper devoted to a team that last played a game half a century ago?)

Just where would baseball get a team? It could create one out of the poor huddled masses of mediocre players yearning for at-bats through expansion, which is precisely how the Mets were born. While some complain that baseball's talent pool is already diluted by the most recent expansions, there is less evidence for this than there is that the Yankee Stadium hot dogs contain ingredients that were at one time meat.

Who says baseball is too diluted? Certainly not the fans in Florida and Arizona who watched their teams beat the Yankees in the 2001 and 2003 World Series, nor the fans throughout the country who were just relieved that some team was finally beating those SOBs. Not the fans who packed the ballparks to watch Bonds, McGwire and Sosa swat home runs in record numbers. And not the fans who delighted at the statistical mastery Randy Johnson and Pedro Martinez enjoyed over their opponents. To the contrary, expansion has increased the enjoyment of fans everywhere, with the obvious exception of Tampa Bay.

Adding a third team to New York is such a simple, sensible plan even Mickey Rivers could instantly grasp it. Unfortunately, it will never happen.

Steinbrenner, like every other owner, can veto any team moving into his market. And Steinbrenner would sooner grow hair down to his shoulders and tattoo "Yankees Suck!" on his bicep than allow another team to come into the New York area and reduce his profits.

That is, unless baseball could convince him such a move would hurt the Mets more than him.

There is one other very obvious downside to this proposal. There would be a third New York–area team that fans elsewhere would wind up hating.

2. End Welfare for the Yankees

Does Burger King ship free meat to McDonald's? Does Coca-Cola reveal its secret formula to Pepsi? Does Nike pay LeBron James $90 million to wear Adidas shoes? Of course not. Why then do so many teams help the Yankees?

Small-market and large-market teams alike complain about the Yankees' competitive advantage, yet most of them turn right around and help New York get even better. As Piniella said before the 2004 season, when it was suggested that the Yankees didn't have enough starting pitching: "So what? George will go out and get some."

Teams sign players to contracts that wind up being too expensive and then they look to the Yankees to take over the contracts. For the sake of a few bucks, they're more than willing to supply arms to the enemy. It's like selling nuclear weapons to North Korea. So many teams call the Yankees when they need to cut payroll that they have Cashman's office number on speed dial. Not that this is a recent development. The Yankees regularly fleeced the Red Sox and owner Harry Frazee in the teens and '20s, acquiring not only Ruth but also Everett Scott, Sad Sam Jones, Bullet Joe Bush, George Pipgras, Ernie Shore, Dutch Leonard, Duffy Lewis, Carl Mays and Herb Pennock. New York also used the Kansas City Athletics as its personal farm team in the 1950s.

Now the Yankees treat the entire major league as their own farm system, so much so that they come to regard other teams' players as their rightful property. When Giambi was riddled by increasing injuries and the club began the 2004 season with concerns in the rotation, the New York media began floating rumors that the Yankees would trade Giambi to the Athletics for Tim Hudson. As soon as Randy Johnson pitched a perfect game, more rumors were printed about New York dealing for the Big Unit.

"It sometimes seems," Diamondbacks general manager Joe Garagiola Jr. complained to ESPN's Jayson Stark, "as if the thought process is: The Yankees have a need. This is the best way to address the need. So let's just do the paperwork and schedule the press conference. It's like the Yankees are the Globetrotters and the rest of us are the Washington Generals."

Especially when the Big Unit told the Diamondbacks that he wanted to be traded to the Yankees. According to the Newark *Star-Ledger*, Johnson's agent told Garagiola, "If you don't trade him to the Yankees, you're going to have one unhappy player." To which Garagiola replied, "And how would I tell the difference?"

While Garagiola and the Diamondbacks resisted the Yankees' call, that summer, the rumors started up again as soon as Kevin Brown walked off the mound in Game 7 of the 2004 ALCS that fall. As Yogi says, it ain't over till it's over. The White Sox did not, dealing them two-time All-Star Esteban Loaiza. Here are some other notorious trades teams have made with the enemy over the years:

Having won their first division title in 1995, the Mariners traded

Tino Martinez and Jeff Nelson to the Yankees for Russ Davis and Sterling Hitchcock. Martinez and Nelson won four World Series rings with the Yankees, while Davis and Hitchcock were flops in Seattle.

The Blue Jays traded Roger Clemens to the Yankees in 1999 after he had just won his second consecutive Cy Young Award in Toronto. Clemens won seventy-seven games, two world championship rings and another Cy Young in New York. The Blue Jays finished in third place the next five seasons.

Midway through the 2000 season, the Yankees needed pitching and left-handed power. The Reds obliged their pitching needs by trading them Denny Neagle, a twenty-game winner, for prospect Drew Henson and three other prospects. With Neagle in the rotation, the Yankees went on to win the division and the World Series. The Reds fell from contention to an also-ran and eventually sent Henson back to New York. In other words, the Reds gave New York a starter in their rotation for almost nothing.

Cleveland took care of the left-handed hitting needs by dealing David Justice to New York for Ricky Ledee, Jake Westbrook and Zach Day. While Westbrook wound up on the 2004 All-Star team, Justice delivered the late homer that sent the Yankees to the World Series in 2000.

The Reds gave the Yankees another handout midway through the 2003 season when they traded All-Star third baseman Aaron Boone to them. Boone, as Red Sox fans recall, played a part in New York's return to the World Series.

Following the season, the Dodgers traded Brown (14-9 with a 2.36 ERA) to the Yankees in exchange for Jeff Weaver (7-9, 5.99 ERA), though based on Brown breaking his hand on the clubhouse wall, the Dodgers did not include his brain.

The Mariners released John Olerud in 2004, allowing the Yankees to sign him for their pennant drive. Because Seattle was still on the hook for his salary, that meant the Mariners were paying Olerud to hit a postseason homer for the Yankees.

The biggest help the Yankees received, of course, was when the Rangers not only traded them A-Rod but also agreed to pay $67 million of his salary as well, reducing Rodriguez's annual cost for New York to about $16 million, or less than they were paying Giambi and Jeter. Rangers owner Tom Hicks had his reasons for making the deal—just as the Judge had his motives for betting against Roy Hobbs and the Knights in *The Natural*—but the effect was that he was subsidizing the richest and best team in baseball so it could put perhaps the best player into the lineup as cheaply as possible.

Sure, the trade wound up helping the Rangers—they received undervalued Alfonso Soriano in exchange—but this strategy still was as shortsighted as giving Emeril Lagasse a prime-time sitcom. It may help a team escape an occasional bad contract but it just makes the Yankees better, which doesn't help anyone in the long run.

This simply must end. The Yankees are always going to be able to sign the marquee free agents they want, but that doesn't mean their rivals have to fill out the rest of the lineup card.

Look, there are twenty-nine other teams besides the Yankees. If you absolutely, positively have to make a trade, deal with one of them, even if you have to eat some of the salary. If you're having trouble making payroll, it's better to bite the bullet and put your expenses on a credit card. Even an 18.3 percent interest rate is preferable to aiding Steinbrenner.

3. Fine-Tune the Luxury Tax

Bob Costas is no rabid Yankee hater. Indeed, he delivered the eulogy at Mantle's funeral. Yet he still sees the need to handicap New York for the sake of the game.

"What is negative is the deck is stacked so much in their favor," he says. "If it was stacked a little bit, and teams had more of a reasonable chance, it would be all to the good. But the way it is now, it's as if one team has nine turns at bat and the others have six.

"That's the problem. Not the history, not the success, not the monuments, not the tradition. You took a team with certain advantages and you amplified them to the point of distortion. They tried with the luxury tax, but what it is working out to be is a salary cap for everyone but the Yankees."

The current system, based loosely on the Monopoly luxury tax model developed by J. P. Moneybags and Parker Brothers, works this way: Teams with payrolls above a certain amount must pay a tax to the league that is then spread among the teams with the lowest payrolls. Because the Yankees are rich enough to pay the tax, Costas says it doesn't slow them from signing players, but it does handicap everyone else.

In other words, while the luxury tax limits other teams, the Yankees are still able to fund their pennant campaigns with soft money. Costas proposes that teams who surpass the luxury tax level should also be prevented from signing or trading for any players who have salaries above a certain level.

"Would that be perceived that the rule is directed specifically at the Yankees? Of course it would," Costas says. "That's certainly how New York fans would see it. But everywhere other than New York, they would think it's a good idea."

4. A Salary Cap with an Officially Licensed Interlocking NY Logo

The salary cap has worked with good success in the NBA and with lesser success in the NFL (where it provides teams with a convenient excuse to cut players, such as the New England Patriots dumping their leading rusher soon after winning the Super Bowl). The possible implementation of a cap has been raised repeatedly in baseball, only to have the players association summarily reject it. And for good reason. One, it is an obvious impediment to salaries, and two, well, the owners proposed it.

Still, the concept has merit, and baseball should make another run at it when the next collective bargaining agreement is up for renewal and everyone starts bitching at each other again.

We need to be realistic about this, though. The players association isn't going to accept any salary cap that will slow salary growth—as strong as the union is, we're lucky they don't demand time and a half for extra innings when the next contract comes up. Which is why the cap would have to be tied to a payroll minimum that teams could not go below, a "salary belt" if you will. The salary cap would restrict a team (i.e., the Yankees) from spending dramatically more money than the rest of the league, while the salary belt would force the cheapest, most miserly team to spend a minimum amount of money on players.

It would be a win-win situation for everyone. The richest teams would have a bit of a handicap, but not a crippling one, and the poorer teams couldn't claim poverty while investing their revenue-sharing checks in tax-free municipal bonds. While some of the elite players may not receive quite as much money as before, they are a minority of the union. The majority of players, however, would see gains in their pay because teams that currently keep their payrolls embarrassingly low would be forced to spend more money. This would reduce the number of players who lose their jobs when they have their contracts nontendered just as they are about to gain some negotiating leverage. If teams had a minimum payroll to meet, they would be much more likely to keep a veteran role player rather than let him go for an untested (and cheap) rookie.

As much as I hate to admit it, Steinbrenner has a legitimate point when he complains that revenue sharing takes money from his team and gives it to owners who simply put it in their wallets without increasing their payrolls at all. "He pays a lot of luxury tax to owners who don't necessarily put it back into their team," Torre correctly points out. The Brewers, despite playing in a new stadium, took in $20 million in revenue sharing in 2004 and yet cut their payroll by $13 million to the lowest in the majors ($27.5 million). It's a wonder they didn't sign Bob Uecker to be their catcher.

The salary cap and salary belt plan would allow revenue sharing to work the way it was intended. It lessens the advantages of the richest teams and makes more frugal teams try harder.

Would the union go for it? Perhaps, but you would have to set the cap and the minimum at agreed-upon percentages of revenue, then allow the union to look at the books (and by that I mean the *real* ones, not the—wink wink—"official" ones) to make sure they're not getting gypped.

5. And If Nothing Else Works

If none of these solutions prove feasible, there are two last hopes for baseball and mankind. One, we can have Jerry Seinfeld tell his pal Superman to fly backward around the earth so that he reverses the planet's orbit and allows us to go back to 1919 and stop the Ruth trade from ever taking place.

Failing that, we can always place the Yankees on the cover of *Sports Illustrated* every week of the season and wait for the jinx to take effect.

Look, I'm not one of those hysterical columnists ranting that low-revenue teams don't have a chance to reach the World Series. The Marlins, Twins and Athletics clearly prove that they can. But it need not be as much of a strain as Michael Moore completing a triathlon, either. By handicapping the Yankees, competing would be easier for everyone involved, while New York would still remain strong enough to inspire sufficiently strong emotions and animosity.

Baseball may not be able to shorten the time of games or stop players from scratching themselves in public, but it can do something about the Yankees. It can recognize the unfair advantages inherent in their location and even things up a bit. It won't be easy but worthwhile things seldom are. If baseball is to keep New York from dominating another century, it needs to address the problem.

The Yankees have ruled the sports world long enough. Just as the government broke up AT&T, it's time for baseball to break up Steinbrenner's evil empire.

Tear down this outfield wall, Mr. Steinbrenner!

So, don't wait for a UN resolution. Forget the French. Now is the time to take preemptive action. Break the chains, storm the barricades, topple the statues in Monument Park, hire Tonya Harding's people to break some kneecaps and fire photon torpedoes into the Death Star's exhaust port. The sooner we can make our ball fields level and free the world from the tyranny of the Yankees, the better. The team has ruined enough seasons by thoughtlessly pricking our gonfalon bubble so often that we become lonely, broken men, so weak and dispirited we're unable to stand up straight in the unemployment line.

Not that I'm bitter or anything.

Unsafe at Any Payroll

For most of his adult life, Ralph Nader dedicated himself to saving the lives of millions of Americans by increasing the safety and reliability of automobiles, cleaning up our water and air and improving working conditions in factories. He also has attempted to clean up government by running for president (with perhaps less impressive results).

But it is only in recent years that he has truly tackled the most serious threats to modern society . . . bitching about the officiating in the NBA and the proliferation of advertising in baseball. The fans' "sense of impartiality and professionalism" was broken by the refs in Game 6 of the 2002 Lakers-Kings playoff series, he wrote David Stern, demanding that the NBA commissioner investigate the controversial calls. "You have sunk to a greedy new low," he wrote Bud Selig after seeing the Yankees and Devil Rays wear ads on their uniforms in Japan in 2004.

Both letters received national attention. Less known was a letter Nader sent to Steinbrenner demanding the Yankees change their ways as well. . . .

Mr. Steinbrenner,

It has come to my attention that your team is in violation of several federal safety, health and pollution standards as specified below.

The New York state health code clearly states that all meat products sold for public consumption must be heated to at least 400 degrees and must be discarded if not sold within thirty-seven minutes of being cooked. You must rectify this situation immediately or we shall be forced to close down your concession stands (not that this would affect service).

Not only has your team won the American League pennant forty times, you recently traded for Alex Rodriguez, the league's most valuable player. Such dominance is in clear violation of the Sherman Antitrust Act of 1890. You are hereby notified that Justice Thomas Penfield Jackson, the U.S. attorney general and the Tampa Bay Devil Rays have ordered the breakup of your monopoly into separate pitching and batting units.

While free speech is constitutionally guaranteed, the court system has consistently upheld community obscenity standards. The fans in the bleachers are in clear violation of these standards and are hereby ordered to alter their language. Suggested alternatives: Darn. Drat. Shoot. Jumping Jehosephat. And of course, Fudge. Also, instead of the offensive and overused "Red Sox suck!" may I suggest, "We respectfully differ with the Red Sox but acknowledge their right to self-determination."

And finally, your bullpen carts do not meet minimum standards for safety, performance, emissions or fuel efficiency. You risk daily fines of $10,000 plus the temporary shutdown of your bullpen if you do not install seat belts immediately and switch to ethanol.

Sincerely,
Ralph Nader

P.S. Ticker-tape parades dump as much as two thousand tons of paper on the streets, straining the city's already strained sanitation crews. Wouldn't it be better if you celebrated by encouraging fans to bring their recyclable materials to the nearest center?

CHAPTER 12

The Ultimate Yankees Quiz

In *The Art of War*, Sun-Tzu wrote that to guarantee victory, you must know your enemy. Do you know enough Yankees history to prepare yourself for battle? Take this quiz and find out.

1. What was the most astounding thing about David Wells's 1998 perfect game?
   A. He wasn't arrested for a DUI when he took the bullpen cart to the mound for the first inning.
   B. He didn't crush catcher Jorge Posada when he leaped into his arms at the end of the game.
   C. He attended the same San Diego high school as Don Larsen, who had thrown the previous perfect game for the Yankees.
   D. He left a few hot dogs for the fans to eat.

Answer: C

2. What happened to little Johnny Sylvester after Babe Ruth slammed the home run he promised to hit for him?
   A. He recovered from a life-threatening injury.
   B. He sold the home run ball on eBay.

   C. He grew up, changed his name to Rudy and was elected mayor of New York.

   D. He died after being kicked out of the hospital for not having insurance.

Answer: A

3. How many times did George Steinbrenner fire Billy Martin?
   A. Four times.
   B. Five times.
   C. Six times.
   D. MIT scientists are still compiling the figure.

Answer: B

4. What did Billy Martin say was the difference between Reggie and Steinbrenner in 1978?
   A. "One's a born liar and the other's convicted."
   B. "One is a pompous, selfish egomaniac who can't play baseball and Steinbrenner is even worse."
   C. "I hate one of them and I would hate the other if I ever gave him any thought at all."
   D. "One is a big fat idiot and the other is just an idiot."

Answer: A

5. Arrange in chronological order:
   A. Steinbrenner fires Billy for the fourth time.
   B. Steinbrenner fires Bill Virdon.
   C. Steinbrenner fires Clyde King.
   D. Steinbrenner fires Dick Howser.
   E. Steinbrenner fires his dietician.

Answer: B, D, C, A, E

6. What was broadcaster Phil Rizzuto's signature line?
   A. "Holy Shit!"
   B. "Holy Cow!"

C. "Holy Mary, Mother of God, Pray for us Yankees!"

D. "Check out the bodacious tah-tahs on that blonde in the third row!"

Answer: B

7. What Yankee Stadium landmark did Roger Clemens rub for luck before each start?

A . The rats under the Yankees bullpen.

B. The bullet holes in the visitors' bullpen.

C. The Ruth monument.

D. The protective cup on the Mantle monument.

Answer: C

8. Which candy bar was named after a Yankee?

A. The $180 Million Payroll Bar

B. The Baby Rudy

C. The Reggie bar

D. The Almonte Joy bar

Answer: C

9. Rank from smallest to largest:

A. Babe Ruth's waistline

B. Reggie Jackson's ego

C. The Yankees' annual payroll

D. Alfonso Soriano's strike zone

Answer: A, D, B, C

10. Why did Lou Gehrig "consider himself the luckiest man on the face of the earth"?

A. Because he had just won the Powerball.

B. Because he was a decent, thoughtful and eloquent man, who, even though he was dying, realized that he had enjoyed a wonderful life, a rewarding career, the love of his family and the support of millions.

C. Because he no longer had to sit next to Bill Dickey and his "lucky underpants."

D. Because he still hadn't made the obvious connection with Lou Gehrig's disease.

Answer: B

11. Reggie Jackson referred to himself as:
    A. The Straw That Stirs the Drink
    B. The Finger That Picks the Nose
    C. The Comb That Styles Mickey Rivers's Hair
    D. The Belt That Holds Up Thurman Munson's Pants

Answer: A

12. Which phrase already associated with Steinbrenner and the Yankees did Donald Trump try to copyright?
    A. Five-peat.
    B. "You're fired."
    C. Red Sox Suck.
    D. Show Your Tits.

Answer: B

13. Which patriotic song do Yankees fans traditionally stand for each game to show their love for this great country?
    A. "God Bless America"
    B. "New York, New York"
    C. "Y.M.C.A."
    D. "Cotton Eye Joe"

Answer: A

14. According to team lore, why do the Yankees wear pinstripes?
    A. They had a slimming effect on Babe Ruth.
    B. To better fit their rich man's image.

C. Brooks Brothers was out of navy double-breasted suits.

D. To hold up their pants.

Answer: A

15. What was Dave Winfield arrested for in Toronto in 1983?
    A. Killing a seagull with a throw
    B. Murdering the Blue Jays pitchers
    C. Killing off a pitcher of LaBatt
    D. Killing another Yankees rally

Answer: A

16. Reggie wears a Yankees cap on his Hall of Fame plaque. Rank the following teams in order of the number of games he played for them, from most to least:
    A. Yankees
    B. Athletics
    C. Angels
    D. Orioles
    E. Mudville Nine

Answer: B, C, A, D, E

17. Contrary to popular belief, what is not in Don Zimmer's head?
    A. Medulla oblongata
    B. Cerebral cortex
    C. Pituitary gland
    D. Steel plate

Answer: D

18. What has never occurred at Yankee Stadium?
    A. No one has ever hit for the cycle.
    B. No one has ever no-hit the Yankees.
    C. No one has ever hit a home run completely out of the stadium.

D. No one has ever sat through an entire game without having something spilled on him.

Answer: C

19. What record does Reggie Jackson hold?
    A. Most career RBIs
    B. Most career errors by a right fielder
    C. Most lifetime strikeouts
    D. Most frequent use of the first person

Answer: C

20. If the No. 4 train leaves Grand Central Station at 6:20 going fifty miles an hour and the B train leaves 42nd Street at 6:34 going forty-five miles an hour and the D express train leaves Columbus Circle at 6:39 going forty-eight miles an hour, which will arrive at Yankee Stadium first?
    A. The 4 train
    B. The B train
    C. The D train
    D. The scalpers demanding $100 for a view-obstructed seat in the upper deck

Answer: C

21. What did Red Sox owner Harry Frazee receive in exchange for Babe Ruth?
    A. $100,000
    B. Fritz Peterson's wife
    C. Thirty pieces of silver
    D. The unending scorn of Boston fans

Answer: A

22. Which of the following numbers so often associated with Yankees players has the team yet to retire?

A. 3
B. 44
C. 7
D. 666

Answer: D

23. What prized Yankees possession did George Costanza drag behind his car in an episode of *Seinfeld*?
   A. The accounting ledger Steinbrenner doesn't show the owners at revenue-sharing time
   B. The steel plate from Zimmer's head
   C. Jeter's little black book
   D. Their 1996 World Series trophy

Answer: D

24. What was the Yankees' first stadium?
   A. The Polo Grounds
   B. Yankee Stadium
   C. Hilltop Park
   D. Hell Field

Answer: C

25. How did Ruth supposedly justify making more money than the president in 1929?
   A. "I have a lot of mistresses and illegitimate kids to take care of."
   B. "I had a better year than he did."
   C. "We live in a society that places too high a value on athletics and too little value on public service."
   D. "Don't worry—this is as high a salary as a baseball player is ever going to get."

Answer: B

How Is Mr. October Chosen?

Mr. October is one of our nation's highest honors, a distinction thus far bestowed on only two players—both Yankees—in all baseball history: Reggie Jackson and Derek Jeter. But how is Mr. October chosen each fall, what are the powers and perks of office and how long may a player serve in office?

The selection process is grueling. According to the Act of Settlement (1701), only players who are the Protestant heirs of Princess Sophia, granddaughter of James I, and *not* on baseball's permanently ineligible list may succeed to the title of Mr. October. In leap years where Punxsutawney Phil sees his shadow and the American League wins the All-Star Game, eligible players campaign in the Iowa Caucus and the March scouting combine. The five candidates who emerge with the most pledged delegates and the highest BCS rankings are placed on the ballot for the Baseball Writers of America Association, the League of Women Voters, the College of Cardinals and members of the Academy of Motion Picture Arts and Sciences. Following the home run derby/debate/swimsuit competition, Rudy Giuliani and Sweden's King Carl Gustaf XVI crown the new Mr. October at a ceremony in Stockholm.

Mr. October holds absolute power over the Bronx during the month's thirty-one days, including specific power to levy taxes, commute prison sentences, call up the National Guard and marry same-sex couples on the subway. Perks of the office include a weekend in Vegas with *Playboy*'s Miss October, a lifetime supply of Reggie bars, a guest appearance on *Letterman*, the eighteenth spot in the line of succession in the British Royal Family (right ahead of His Royal Highness, Prince Richard, the second Duke of Gloucester) and free cable.

Plus, Mr. Met has to get his coffee.

The 20th Amendment prohibits any player from serving as Mr. October for a span that covers the release of more than two Kevin Costner baseball movies.

Should a Mr. October be unable to fulfill his duties for any reason, the official line of succession is as follows:

1. Mr. Coffee
2. Mr. Cub
3. Mr. Met
4. Mrs. Fields
5. Miss Manners
6. Mr. Bubble
7. Mister Magoo
8. Mr. Greenjeans
9. The Famous Chicken
10. The Secretary of Agriculture

26. Yogi Berra served in what legendary battle?
    A. The Battle of the Bulge
    B. D-day
    C. Midway
    D. Billy Martin's barroom brawl at Lace

Answer: B (but we'll also accept D)

27. Steinbrenner was born on what celebrated date in U.S. history?
    A. Thanksgiving Day
    B. The Fourth of July
    C. Labor Day
    D. A date which will live in infamy

Answer: B (but we'll also accept D)

28. Arrange from shortest to longest:
    A. The lines at Yankee Stadium's concession stands
    B. The lines at Yankee Stadium's bathrooms

C. The distance to the right field corner

D. Oscar Gamble's hair

Answer: D, B, A, C

29. What did Texas Rangers owner Tom Hicks receive in exchange for Alex Rodriguez in 2004?

A. Manny Ramirez

B. Alfonso Soriano

C. Alfonso Soriano and a player to be named later

D. Thousands of death threats from Red Sox Nation

Answer: C

30. What was the New York *Daily News* headline when the Yankees hired Joe Torre?

A. "Yanks Hire Frank's Brother"

B. "The Next Victim"

C. "Clueless Joe"

D. "Who?"

Answer: C

31. In the musical *Damn Yankees*, what does Joe Boyd sell so that the Washington Senators will finally win the pennant?

A. A Wayne Terwilliger rookie card

B. His pocket watch and his wife's hair

C. His immortal soul to the devil

D. Crack cocaine to D.C. mayor Marion Berry

Answer: C

32. What is inscribed on the Lou Gehrig plaque in Monument Park?

A. "Despite what he said, apparently he wasn't *really* the luckiest man in the world."

B. "Cal Ripken Jr. couldn't hold his jockstrap."

C. "A man, a gentleman and a great player whose amazing record of 2,130 consecutive games should stand for all time."

D. "A man, a gentleman and a great player whose amazing record of 2,130 consecutive games should stand for all time. Either that or about fifty-six years."

Answer: C

33. Match the Yankees greats in the first column with their unofficial nicknames in the second:

A.	Hideki Irabu	I.	Mr. May
B.	Ed Whitson	II.	The Gerbil
C.	Dave Winfield	III.	E-4
D.	Chuck Knoblauch	IV.	The Ol' Four-Finger Discount
E.	Bucky Dent	V.	The San Diego Chicken
F.	Ruben Rivera	VI.	The Shame of St. Mary's School for Teenage Girls
G.	Luis Polonia	VII.	Dr. Feelgood
H.	Steve Howe	VIII.	The Fat Pussy Toad
I.	Don Zimmer	IX.	Bucky "#$%&ing" Dent

Answer: A-VIII, B-V, C-I, D-III, E-IX, F-IV, G-VI, H-VII, I-II

34. What was Babe Ruth's famous "called shot"?

A. A home run off Carl Hubbell in the 1935 All-Star Game

B. A home run in his final major league at-bat

C. A home run off Charlie Root in the 1932 World Series

D. Usually bourbon but occasionally scotch

Answer: C

35. Which was not a nickname of Lou Gehrig?

A. Larruppin' Lou

B. The Columbia Engineer

C. The King of Pop

D. Old Biscuit Pants

Answer: C

36. What did Billy Martin say was wrong with George Brett's bat in a 1983 game?

A. It had "Wonderboy" burned into its barrel.

B. It was corked.

C. It had too much pine tar on the handle.

D. It had been autographed by Joe DiMaggio at a card show when DiMaggio very clearly announced he was only signing flat items.

Answer: C

37. Which TV network owned the Yankees from 1964 to 1973?

A. NBC

B. CBS

C. ABC

D. Comedy Central

Answer: B

38. What is not the title of a movie about the Yankees?

A. *Pride of the Yankees*

B. *61**

C. *Damn Yankees*

D. *The Scout*

E. *@#&*ing Yankees!!!*

Answer: E

39. Who did Chuck Knoblauch hit with a bad throw into the stands in 2000?

A. Mike Piazza

B. Keith Olbermann's mother

C. John Sterling's cousin twice removed
D. Mayor Giuliani's mistress

Answer: B

40. What was the name of the Yankees before they became the Yankees?
A. Murderers Boulevard
B. The Bronx Farmers
C. The Highlanders
D. The Candy Stripers

Answer: C

41. What postseason umpiring blunder did the Yankees not benefit from during their 1996–2003 championship era?
A. Rich Garcia not noticing that Jeffrey Maier reached out and interfered with a fly ball in the 1996 playoffs.
B. Tim Tschida assuming that Knoblauch tagged a base runner in the 1999 playoffs.
C. Rich Garcia calling what should have been strike three a ball just before Tino Martinez hit a game-winning grand slam in the 1998 World Series.
D. Don Denkinger ruling that Claudell Washington was safe at first base in the 2000 World Series to keep a game-winning rally alive even though he had been retired for fourteen years.

Answer: D

42. What was infielder Phil Linz playing when he got in trouble on the team bus in 1964?
A. A harmonica
B. Tenor sax
C. Harpsichord
D. Strip poker

Answer: A

43. While working as the Yankees assistant traveling secretary, what does George Costanza get Steinbrenner addicted to?
    A. Black tar heroin
    B. Tobacco
    C. Calzones
    D. Fenway franks

Answer: C

44. Why was Steinbrenner given a two-year ban from baseball shortly after buying the Yankees in 1973?
    A. He made illegal campaign contributions to Richard Nixon.
    B. He made illegal contributions to the Winfield Foundation.
    C. He bet on the Reds.
    D. Incredible foresight on the part of commissioner Bowie Kuhn.

Answer: A (but we'll also accept D)

45. What did YES broadcaster Michael Kay call a "disgrace" in 2004?
    A. The Yankees $196 million payroll
    B. Alex Rodriguez's $252 million contract
    C. Johnny Damon's long hair
    D. Beer prices at Yankee Stadium

Answer: C

46. What was Joe DiMaggio's nickname?
    A. The Yankee Clipper
    B. The Queen Mary
    C. The 5:15 Local to Poughkeepsie
    D. The Connecticut Yankee in Bea Arthur's Pants

Answer: A

47. Who did Gehrig replace when he started his 2,130-game playing streak?

A. Ruth
B. Wally Pipp
C. "Pee-Wee" Wanninger
D. "Disabled List" Crosetti

Answer: B

48. Which is not an actual Yogi-ism?
    A. "When you come to a fork in the road, take it."
    B. "It ain't over 'til it's over."
    C. "It gets late early here."
    D. "You can lead a horse to water but you can't leave him un-locked outside Yankee Stadium or someone will steal him."

Answer: D

49. What were Ruth's last words?
    A. "Are you going to eat the rest of that?"
    B. "I'm going over the valley."
    C. "Pass me the bottle opener."
    D. "How do you unhook this bra?"

Answer: B

50. What do the Bleacher Creatures in right field do during the tra-ditional roll call in the first inning?
    A. They chant each Yankee starter's name until the player ac-knowledges them.
    B. They beat up each fan rooting for the opposing team until the fan begs for mercy.
    C. They chant that each opposing starter sucks until the player breaks down and cries.
    D. They pass out in the gutter.

Answer: A

Scoring key:

45–50: They replaced MSG with YES Network on your cable package, too, huh?

35–44: You probably studied up for the quiz while stuck in Big Dig construction traffic.

25–34: You likely have a nice, well-rounded life, other than the fact that your car radio occasionally gets stuck on John Sterling.

15–24: You don't live anywhere near the Yankees' influence and probably don't understand the English language.

5–14: Let me guess—you're a Mets fan, right?

0–4: Congratulations, Mr. Wells. You really improved over your previous test.

Amazing Non-Yankees Feats

In 1926, the Babe visited a dying child in a hospital and promised to hit a home run for him during the World Series. He not only hit one home run, he hit four, and little Johnny Sylvester miraculously recovered thanks to these heroics. Except that's not exactly how it happened, according to Robert Creamer's definitive biography on Ruth, *Babe: The Legend Comes to Life*. In Creamer's account, Sylvester was hospitalized after being badly hurt falling off a horse. A family friend brought the boy several autographed balls before the World Series, plus a promise from Ruth that he would homer for the kid. Babe only visited Sylvester after the series had already been played.

Sylvester's uncle met Ruth the following spring, thanked him and told him that Johnny had recovered and was doing well. "That's good," Ruth said. "Give him my regards."

Creamer wrote that Ruth watched the man walk away and said, "Now, who in the hell is Johnny Sylvester?"

Until 2004, the Yankees had always gotten the best of the Red Sox when a championship was on the line, right? Well, not always. In 1904, the Yankees and the defending world champion Red Sox battled for the pennant for the first time. New York's corrupt owners tipped the race in Boston's favor when they decided weeks in advance to rent out their stadium, Hilltop Park, for the final Saturday of the season. That meant that with the pennant on the line, what should have been a home game was played in Boston the final weekend. And the Red Sox beat the Yankees that day, helping them win the pennant.

In Game 3 of the 1932 series, Ruth responded to vicious taunting and heckling by pointing to the center field bleachers before a pitch to "call his shot"—that he would hit the next pitch from Charlie Root to that spot for a home run. And then he did, providing baseball with one of the greatest moments in its history. Or did he? This was years before Tim McCarver was born to belabor every point in the World Series, and with no instant replays, the called shot has been an issue of debate for decades. While it's generally undisputed that Ruth made some sort of gesture to the Cubs, Root always claimed Ruth did not call his shot, while the Babe's story constantly changed. In *Yankees Century*, Glenn Stout writes that only one reporter, Joe Williams, referred to it as a called shot in the next day's paper, but that as the days passed more and more writers began describing it that way. "Most mirrored Williams's account, and none debunked it as pure hokum." Fortunately, a 16mm film shot by Harold Warp was discovered more than sixty years later, and as Stout writes, "the film clearly demonstrates that Ruth didn't point to center and he never called his shot."

How did the tape-measure home run originate? As everyone knows, it was after Mantle slammed a home run out of Washington's Griffith Stadium in 1953 and Yankees PR man Red Patterson measured the home run off at 565 feet with a tape measure. Well, that may be when the phrase originated, but Patterson later admitted that he never used a tape measure to measure the home run. According to Stout's *Yankees Century*, he simply asked a kid outside the stadium where the ball landed and guessed.

Until McGwire, Sosa and Bonds came along, what was the record for most home runs in a 162-game season? Yankees fans and almost everyone else will tell you it was sixty-one, by Roger Maris in 1961. Which technically isn't quite correct. Even with all the controversy over whether there should have been an asterisk next to Maris's name since he needed more than 154 games to break Babe Ruth's mark, it is usually forgotten that Maris hit his sixty-first home run in what was actually New York's 163rd game. That's because the Yankees had a game rained out April 22 with the score tied 5–5. Even though the tie was not reflected in the standings, the individual performances in the game were counted in the record book.

CHAPTER 13

The Devil Wears Pinstripes

O f course, these is one other solution to the Yankees dilemma that I didn't go into in Chapter 12. . . .

The Devil Wears Pinstripes

A PLAY IN ONE ACT

The curtain opens on the Seventh Level of Hell, where lava flows and stalactites glow red from the ever-present fires of Hades. Serpents wriggle across the floor while the anguished cries of doomed souls and the smell of brimstone fills the air.

Much of the stage is filled with row upon row of telephone solicitors. We hear them chatter as the stage lights brighten.

PHONE SOLICITOR #10   But with our great introductory credit card, we can lower your interest rate to 8.3 percent for the first forty-eight hours and just 28.8 percent above prime after that . . .

PHONE SOLICITOR #234   Congratulations, you've just won a weekend in Reno, and all you have to do is sit through three brief, low-pressure, virtually no-obligation, fourteen-hour time-share presentations . . .

PHONE SOLICITOR #3,368,234   Well, I'm sure your parents would love to have a new satellite dish so you can watch SpongeBob SquarePants even more than you do now. We have a truck in your neighborhood this afternoon and if you just say yes for Mommy and Daddy, they would be happy to drop by. No, no need to bother them—I'm sure they're busy. Just say yes now and you'll have 250 channels by this afternoon . . .

(As the PHONE SOLICITORS *continue their business, a spotlight follows a lone figure walking hesitantly among the desks. He is our hero,* SCOOTER THOMAS, *a middle-aged baseball fan wearing a battered, sweat-stained Montreal Expos cap. He has journeyed to Hell on a dangerous but urgent personal mission.*

SCOOTER *finds himself center stage at the massive desk of a horrible, horned creature with red, scaly flesh, an outlandish Fu Manchu, a long pointy tail and a pitchfork. He is eating flies from a jar.*

SCOOTER   Hey, I recognize you. You're Scott Boras.

SECRETARY   No, but I get that all the time. I'm Satan's personal, private executive secretary. Do you have an appointment to see the Prince of Darkness?

SCOOTER   No, but I would like to speak to him. It's rather urgent. My name is Scooter Thomas and I've come all the way from Washington, D.C.

SECRETARY   You're in luck. The Master's calendar is rather free at the moment. If you'll just take a spot on the roasting spit, I think he can see you in 327 years, 8 months and 13 days.

SCOOTER   What? I can't wait that long. Isn't there any way you can squeeze me in earlier?

SECRETARY   Well, let me look.

As the SECRETARY *thumbs through the calendar, the* DEVIL *enters stage left, meticulously dressed in a pin-striped business suit. He slaps* SO-LICITOR #3,368,234 *on the back as he passes him.*

DEVIL   I liked that angle where you break down weeping and say that your son has leukemia and you need the commission from your telephone sales to pay for his treatment. Very good, very creative. You must have been a car salesman. Keep it up—remember, for every sale you make, I lower the heat in your cave by 1/10,000th of a degree.

The DEVIL *stops by his* SECRETARY's *desk and grabs the mail.*

DEVIL   Any messages while I was out?

SECRETARY   Just the usual, Boss. The doomed souls of the Second Circle say the bristles on their toothbrushes have worn out and they won't be able to finish scrubbing the latrines until they get new ones. The damned on the Fourth Level say the boulder they have to repeatedly roll to the top of Mount Doom is beginning to chip and become lopsided. Traffic is still snarled along the River Styx due to all the entrance ramp meters you installed.

Oh, and the Hussein brothers are complaining again that the air conditioners still don't work in their cavern.

DEVIL   Tell Uday and Qusay that I personally guarantee plant maintenance will have all the air conditioners working by this Friday at the latest.

SECRETARY   Really?

DEVIL   No, of course not.

SECRETARY   (*Laughing*) You're the best, Boss, the absolute best.

DEVIL   (*Pointing to* SCOOTER) Who's he?

SCOOTER   My name's Scooter Thomas and I've come to see you all the way from Washington, D.C.

DEVIL   Washington? What, is it election season again already?

SCOOTER   No, I'm not a politician—I'm a baseball fan. A very big baseball fan. And I think I have a proposition that just may interest you.

DEVIL   All right, all right. C'mon in. (*Whispering to the* SECRETARY) Be sure to buzz me in ten minutes so I can get rid of him.

(*The* DEVIL *climbs a circular staircase leading to his opulent office, filled with autographed photos of himself shaking hands with various politicians, totalitarian despots, Fortune 500 CEOs and Oprah. He takes his seat behind his desk and begins uploading computer viruses onto the Internet.* SCOOTER *follows and takes a seat.*)

DEVIL   Well, what do you want? Speak up. I don't have much time. This is the busiest part of the year for me.

SCOOTER   Easter?

DEVIL   No, TV's spring sweeps. Now, tell me what this is about or I'll tell Stalin and Jeffrey Dahmer they have a new roommate.

SCOOTER   OK, I'll get right to the point. I'd like to sell you my soul so that the Washington Senators can beat the Yankees and win the pennant.

DEVIL   The Washington Senators? What in Hell are you talking about? The Senators aren't in Washington anymore. They moved to Minnesota in 1961. And after they put in an expansion team in D.C., those other Senators moved to Texas in 1972.

SCOOTER   That's true, but major league baseball is moving the Expos to Washington and if so, I didn't want to have to wait around watching a bad team for a couple years. So I'm offering my soul now for a pennant in their first year.

DEVIL   No. I already did that exact same thing once and it didn't work out.

SCOOTER   Oh, you mean the Senators winning the pennant despite your plan to have the Yankees win anyway and then the guy getting to keep his soul in the end?

DEVIL   No, I mean they made it into a musical.

(The SECRETARY *buzzes the* DEVIL *on the intercom.)*

SECRETARY   Boss, the president of the International Brotherhood of Disembowelers, Eye-Pluckers and Department of Motor Vehicle Workers, Local 487 is here again. He insists that his union members are entitled to overtime pay if they put in more than 167 hours in a week.

DEVIL   No, they're not. They only get time and a half if they put in more than 167 hours a week for more than 3,856 consecutive years and only if they have signed approval from three supervisors. The rules are very clear on overtime in eternity. Tell him it's covered right in section 213, subsection 762E, clause 21H, paragraph W, line 9,403 of the Eternal Damnation Code, right next to the rules on the capital gains tax cuts.

   Oh, and while you're at it, tell him I'm raising the co-pay on medical exams again.

(The DEVIL *turns back to* SCOOTER *and gestures dismissively.)*

DEVIL   Unions.

   Now where was I?

SCOOTER   You were saying you didn't like *Damn Yankees*.

DEVIL   No, that's not right. It's musicals in general I don't like. They're all so sickeningly sentimental, good-spirited and nice. Take *Sound of Music*. Way too many kids, not nearly enough Nazis.

But *Damn Yankees* was all right, I suppose. I was just uncomfortable with its image of Satan, the Dark Prince, the Lord of the Flies, the Father of Lies, the Prime Minister of Parking Meter Maids—to show me singing, dancing, laughing and cracking jokes on stage? It was insulting. Why couldn't they have had me do something uplifting, like bursting out of a batboy's stomach and devouring the umpire's head?

SCOOTER   I see your point.

DEVIL   I did have a good idea about a remake, though. Instead of casting me as the singing and dancing villain, it would have been Steinbrenner. Tom Hicks and the A-Rod trade even inspired me to update the song "Whatever Lola Wants." Listen.

(The DEVIL *begins singing to the tune "Whatever Lola Wants.")*

Whoever Georgie wants
Georgie swipes
And li'l Ranger, Georgie wants A-Rod
You better believe all the hypes
I don't want to hear any gripes
He's already been fitted with pinstripes
Give in . . .

Whoever Georgie wants
Georgie starts gripping
And li'l owner, Georgie wants A-Rod
It's a fate you won't be skipping
Best just accept your whipping
Be happy I don't stick you with the charges for shipping
Give in . . .

Whoever Georgie wants
Georgie skims
And li'l Hicksie, Georgie wants A-Rod
I'm extending your October famines
Making you swim upstream like salmons
The deal is already done, says Gammons
Give in . . .

SCOOTER Very nice.

DEVIL I thought so, too. But I couldn't get the rights. The only show any producer offered me was *Cats* and not even I would have made people suffer through that.

SCOOTER Look, I promise you there will be no musical this time. This deal will be strictly between you and me. No one else will ever be the wiser.

DEVIL Sorry, I'm out of the soul-buying business. Now, if you would kindly close the door on your way out, I have to some extremely important computer transactions to make.

(The DEVIL turns back to his computer, touches his keyboard and sends nine penile-enlargment ads to every e-mail address in the world.)

SCOOTER Wait a minute. What do you mean you don't buy souls anymore? Everyone knows that's how it works. It's how you keep Hell filled with souls. It's a time-honored plot device in literature and film. Besides, how would you keep things going here without the buying and selling of souls? I mean, the heating bills alone must be outrageous.

DEVIL Wise up, buddy. Buying souls simply got much too expensive and too difficult. Athletes don't want to sell their souls when it's easier to buy steroids. Politicians would rather take soft money and use

527 committees for their dirty work. Entertainers always make you deal with their agents—and those bloodsuckers want a 15 percent cut. I tell you, I've got a special Circle of Hell reserved for agents.

Besides, it was too risky. The last soul I bought was Ben Affleck, and I regret that purchase every time he makes a movie. That's what really swore me off the soul-buying thing. I mean, after *Gigli, Surviving Christmas* and *Jersey Girl*, go on, I don't think I want to collect on his soul anyway. Like I want to listen to him whine about the Red Sox all eternity. The doomed souls may have to suffer the rest of their days in 450-degree heat while pitchfork-wielding demons hang them by their entrails and roast them on a spit, but some things are just cruel and unusual punishment.

SCOOTER   So if you don't buy souls, how does it work around here?

DEVIL   Believe me, I still keep my hands in. But instead of buying souls directly, I outsource them.

For instance, in the past if I wanted to buy a politician's soul, I would have to visit Washington, schedule an appointment, take him out to dinner, tempt him with women, wine, drugs and defense contracts—and none of that comes cheap, let me assure you. But I avoided all that hassle by just buying the NRA, the tobacco industry and a couple other lobbies and letting them do all the heavy lifting. The Enron accountants insist it's a better allocation of resources while my lawyers assure me that I'm not nearly as exposed to liability issues this way. It works pretty well. We're even thinking of going public next year. *(He leans over the desk and whispers conspiratorially to* SCOOTER.*)* I must say, the possibilities for insider-trading are very exciting.

(The DEVIL *turns back to his computer, taps a key and sends twelve appeals for money for an exiled Rwandan prince to every e-mail address in the world.)*

SCOOTER   So there's absolutely no way I could convince you to buy my soul so my baseball team could win the World Series?

DEVIL   Afraid not. Even if I were still in that line of work, I wouldn't do it.

SCOOTER   Why not?

DEVIL   I own the Yankees.

(The DEVIL *taps a key on his computer and sends twenty-one mortgage-refinancing ads to every e-mail address in the world.)*

SCOOTER   Hold on. I thought Steinbrenner owned the Yankees.

DEVIL   George? Don't be ridiculous. He's just the front man.

You see, that whole *Damn Yankees* thing got me thinking. Why shouldn't the Lord of the Dead and the Source of All Evil have control of the Yankees? Just think of the exposure and influence they would provide me. The branding and marketing possibilities are endless.

Besides, I always wanted to sit in a luxury suite.

So I decided to take things into my own hands by buying the Yankees when CBS put them up for sale in 1973. But in order to gain approval from the rest of the owners, I bought them by using Steinbrenner. He was an assistant in his dad's shipbuilding business and looking to make a big splash, so he never even questioned where the money was coming from. Same thing when I told him he needed to write those checks to Nixon's slush fund. I told him the money was going to the NYPD Widows and Orphans Fund.

SCOOTER   So, you're the real owner of the Yankees? The man who's responsible for everything they've done in the past thirty years?

DEVIL   No, not everything. I refuse to take the blame for the Hideki Irabu signing. Or *Yankeeography.*

But the Bucky Dent home run, the Jeffrey Maier home run, the Mike Piazza beaning, the Derek Jeter shovel pass, the home runs off Byung-Hyun Kim, Grady Little's brain lock, the Alex Rodriguez trade, the bleacher creatures, high beer prices, advertising on the uniforms in Japan—you name it, if it helped the Yankees, I made it all happen.

And it's not just the Yankees. I was responsible for Albert Belle, the 1981 strike, the old Padres uniforms, dancing groundskeepers, "Who Let the Dogs Out," personal-seat licenses and the Bartman play, too.

SCOOTER You caused Bartman to reach out and interfere with that foul pop? You made the Cubs blow a three-run lead and miss the World Series in 2003? Why would you do such a thing? I can understand making Grady stick with Pedro so you could beat the Red Sox, but how would the Cubs reaching the World Series have hurt the Yankees?

DEVIL It wouldn't have hurt the Yankees. But I had to stop the Cubs to keep Hell running smoothly. Ice floes had already begun forming on the River Styx.

(The SECRETARY interrupts by buzzing the DEVIL on the intercom.)

SECRETARY Boss, telephone solicitor #4,722,821 wants to know whether he should be asking for donations to the Republicans or the Democrats.

DEVIL Both! Doesn't anybody read the employee training manuals anymore? (The DEVIL shakes his head, shrugs and returns his attention to SCOOTER.) It's so hard to find competent evil souls these days.

SCOOTER Amazing. You own the Yankees and no one suspects a thing.

DEVIL Well, that's not entirely true. There were some suspicions that one time when Don Zimmer's head spun around and spewed green vomit. But most people simply assumed that he was just really, really mad at Pedro Martinez.

SCOOTER Still, I don't get it. If you own the team, why do the Yankees ever lose? Why did they blow that 3–0 lead in 2004?

DEVIL   What, you think I can work miracles whenever I want? As much as I hate to admit it, there is a higher power that even I must answer to.

SCOOTER   God?

DEVIL   No, revenue sharing. I can deal with God. But the commissioner's office? Ughhhh. But we all have our cross to bear.

Still, I endure. And it's not so bad. Every time the commissioner asks for more money, I just raise the ticket prices again.

(Crestfallen, SCOOTER *shakes his head and stares at the floor. The* DEVIL *presses the intercom.)*

DEVIL   Before I forget, call the florist and send a nice bouquet to Ken Lay. I want to let him know he's still in my thoughts.

SCOOTER   *(Trying one last time)* And you really don't buy any souls anymore?

DEVIL   How many times do I have to tell you? No! Sheesh—and I thought Kevin Brown had a thick skull when he smashed his hand against the clubhouse wall. Now, leave me alone. I've got a full workload in the Middle East.

SCOOTER   OK, OK. I guess I'll be leaving.

DEVIL   Good. On your way out, tell my secretary to have personnel dock Cratchit's pay again.

SCOOTER   But answer me one last thing. You own just a few influential government lobbies and you run   Yankees. Is that really enough to fund Hell and keep your operation going for all eternity?

DEVIL   Oh, no. Of course not. I also own Ticketmaster.

Curtain

SUGGESTED READING

In addition to a lifetime of rooting against the Yankees and nearly two decades covering baseball professionally, I made use of many very enjoyable works on the team. Although buying these books was occasionally embarrassing at the checkout counter—*"No, really, I'm not a Yankees fan. These four volumes on Mickey Mantle are just for research for a book I'm writing. Trust me, I don't like the Yankees. Honest. Just take my credit card. And could you wrap them in brown paper?"*—they were a wonderful research aid. All are recommended—even for readers who don't like the Yankees.

Glenn Stout's thorough *Yankees Century* is written with the Yankees fan in mind but doesn't shy from bringing up many of the lesser moments in franchise history. Even Red Sox fans would enjoy it—though they probably prefer Stout's *Red Sox Century*.

For a history of Steinbrenner and the team under his ownership up to his 1991 suspension, you can't beat the terrifically entertaining *Damned Yankees* by Bill Madden and Moss Klein—I can't recommend it highly enough. Dick Schaap's *Steinbrenner!* likewise is a superb biography. Neil Sullivan's *The Diamond in the Bronx* is a meticulously researched and very readable history of Yankee Stadium. *Those Damn Yankees* by Dean Chadwin is a penetrating examination of the team's seamier side that Yankees fans no doubt would prefer burned than read. John Helyar gives a great and very balanced look at Steinbrenner in his page-turning *Lords of the Realm* on baseball's owners.

Richard Ben Cramer's *Joe DiMaggio* is a riveting and damning biography on Joltin' Joe (and do yourself a favor by getting a copy of his *What Do You Think of Ted Williams Now?*, perhaps the best portrait I've ever read on anyone). David Halberstam's bestseller, *Summer of '49,* is a loving and engrossing recount of that year's pennant race. Robert Creamer's *Babe: The Legend Comes to Life* is a terrific biography of the best player in the game's history.

Jim Reisler's *Before They Were the Bombers* is a valuable look at an often neglected period of Yankees history. Peter Golenbock's *Dynasty* and Maury Allen's *All Roads Lead to October* provide rich detail on the 1949–64 and 1973–2000 Yankees, respectively.

Now Pitching for the Yankees by Marty Appel is a good look at what it's like to work for the Yankees by their former public relations director of the same name. Jerome Holtzman's *No Cheering in the Press Box* is a marvelous oral history of the early decades of sportswriting (the only shame is Jerome doesn't tell stories from his own career). *Baseball's Great Experiment* by historian Jules Tygiel is the authoritative—and immensely readable—account of Jackie Robinson breaking the color line.

Jim Bouton's *Ball Four* remains the best book ever written about baseball and fully deserving of its spot on the New York Public Library's 100 Most Important Books of the Twentieth Century. David Falkner's *The Last Yankee* is as good a biography of Bill Martin as you can hope to find. Mickey Mantle's many collaborations, *My Favorite Summer*

1956, *All My Octobers* and *The Mick* are all entertaining recounts of what it was like to be an athletic hero in New York (and what it was like to play for George Weiss). *Perfect I'm Not* is supposedly by David Wells.

Baseball's Greatest Quotations, collected by Paul Dickson, and *Voices of Baseball*, collected by Bob Chieger, are always within easy reach of my research library, as are *Rob Neyer's Big Book of Baseball Lineups*, *Bill James Historical Baseball Abstract*, several editions of *The Baseball Encyclopedia* by Macmillan Publishing, *Total Baseball* by John Thorn et al. and *The Encyclopedia of Baseball* by David and Michael Neft and Richard Cohen. The Yankees annual media guide is also a useful research tool.

And finally, I would like to recommend John Steinbeck's *East of Eden*, Yann Martel's *Life of Pi*, Doris Kearns Goodwin's *No Ordinary Time* and Charles Dickens's *Great Expectations*. Not only are they all wonderful books, they don't have a thing to do with the Yankees.